Introduction to
Results-Oriented Management and Accountability (ROMA)

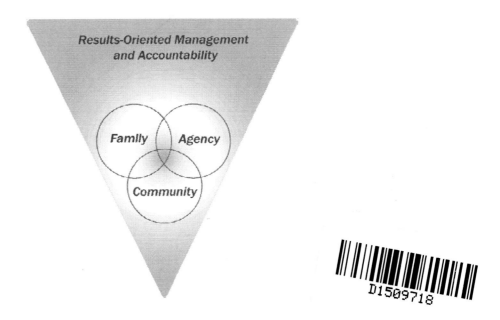

Frederick Richmond
The Center for Applied Management Practices, Inc.

Barbara Mooney
National Peer-to-Peer ROMA Training and Certification Project

Introduction to Results-Oriented Management and Accountability
for
Community Action Agencies and
CSBG Eligible Entities

5.0 Participant Manual
August 2012

"Introduction to ROMA" was adapted from material developed by Frederick Richmond, CEO, The Center for Applied Management Practices, Inc. (CAMP) in the early 1990s. In 1998, Richmond's work became a part of a Train-the-Trainer project known as the "Virtual Outcomes College," under the direction of John Wilson, Executive Director of the Community Action Association of Pennsylvania (CAAP).

The material has been modified many times over the years based on our observations of practices in the Community Service Block Grant (CSBG) network and on changes in practices and policies at the Federal level. Changes have also been made as a result of feedback and input from National Certified ROMA Trainers across the country. It is now is a collaboration between Richmond and Dr. Barbara Mooney, Project Director of the National Peer-to-Peer ROMA Training and Certification Project.

Foundational work by Richmond and other leaders, such as Reginald Carter, Peter Drucker, and Joseph Wholey, continue to support our evolving understanding of the principles and practices of ROMA.

For more information, see the following web sites:

www.appliedmgt.com
The Center for Applied Management Practices, Inc.

www.roma-nptp.org
National Peer-to-Peer ROMA Training and Certification Project

www.ANCRT.org
Association of National Certified ROMA Trainers

An Introduction to the Writings of Peter F. Drucker and Reginald K. Carter

In our *Introduction to ROMA* we use two management methodologies to build a foundation for implementation of ROMA: the **Drucker Questions** from the *Drucker Foundation Self Assessment Workbook* and the **Seven Key Questions** from Reginald Carter's *The Accountable Agency.*

Peter Drucker, sometimes referred to as the world's most recognized management consultant, provides us with a framework for considering the overall management of the agency. The Carter material extends the framework by providing us with accountability questions.

The *Drucker Foundation Self-Assessment Participant Workbook,* or *Drucker Foundation Workbook* first published in 1999 is introduced into the ROMA curriculum to reinforce the concept that ROMA is part of the generally accepted management process and the on-going delivery of human services and these same factors apply to the implementation and administration of ROMA tools and practices.

Management theory as we know it today was originally designed for government and nonprofit institutions at the turn of the century, most notably in 1901 for the U. S Army and later in 1912 for the nonprofit Mayo Clinic. It found its way into the for-profit sector in the 1930s during the Great Depression. The use of these practices and the use of outcomes are a return "to their roots."

The five Drucker questions are presented throughout the material to contextualize ROMA implementation in sound management practices.

The Seven Key Questions were first published by Sage Publications in 1983 in a book written by Reginald K. Carter entitled, *The Accountable Agency. At* the time of publication, Mr. Carter was the Director of Planning and Evaluation for the Michigan Department of Social Services. Together with Harry Hatry of the Urban Institute in Washington D.C., he developed what later became known as Client Outcome Monitoring, one of the predecessors of ROMA. In 1981, Carter and Hatry co-authored a book entitled, *Developing Client Outcome Monitoring Systems: A Guide for State and Local Social Service Agencies.*

When Carter developed the seven key questions for *The Accountable Agency,* he prefaced it with the following paragraph, " Each year when a program manager presents a request for funds, there are seven key questions that legislators, funding agencies, and top administrators should ask:" These questions are as relevant today as they were in 1983 and are at the core of agency and program accountability.

Table of Contents

Participant Manual, "Introduction to ROMA" Version 5.0 © 2012 F. Richmond and B. Mooney, The Center for Applied
Management Practices. Modified, from material © 1997- 2011, The Center for Applied Management Practices. Camp Hill,
PA 717-730-3705, www.appliedmgt.com.

Module Six – Observing Achievement of Results Using Outcome Scales and Matrices **77**

Module Seven – Managing Performance with the Logic Model **95**

Closing **117**

Ten Questions

Please circle either "True" or "False" for each of the questions below.

1. True or False: Community Action agencies (CAAs) most effectively evaluate their results by focusing on the activities supported exclusively by the Community Services Block Grant (CSBG).

2. True or False: CSBG funds are a dedicated funding stream to support the work of Community Action.

3. True or False: "ROMA" is the term for the required reporting of data to a state and the Federal government.

4. True or False: CAAs are expected to focus on moving individuals and families to self-sufficiency and on community transformation, in addition to providing services to low-income people.

5. True or False: CAA programs are designed so that clients who participate in their services achieve measurable results.

6. True or False: Analysis of the agency's results can be used to identify effectiveness and performance of an agency.

7. True or False: The use of "results" instead of "services" may reduce the agency's competitiveness and marketability because of low numbers of results reported.

8. True or False: Community Action Agencies select services to offer based on available funding, not necessarily on the identified community needs.

9. True or False: "Results Oriented Management and Accountability" (ROMA) is the CAA term for a range of agency operation and administrative activities in addition to reporting.

10. True or False: Implementing ROMA in your CAA will affect the planning and fiscal functions, but will not affect the way programs and services are delivered.

Participant Manual, "Introduction to ROMA" Version 5.0 © 2012 F. Richmond and B. Mooney, The Center for Applied Management Practices. Modified, from material © 1997- 2011, The Center for Applied Management Practices. Camp Hill, PA 717-730-3705, www.appliedmgt.com.

Module One

History, Purpose, and Perspective

Learning Objectives:

- Participants will be able to identify historical milestones of Community Action and understand how these relate to ROMA implementation.

- Participants will learn that Community Action Agencies, with a focus on family, agency and community outcomes, have always been designed to be more than simply direct service providers.

- Participants will understand how lessons from history can help us identify future actions.

Participant Manual, "Introduction to ROMA" Version 5.0 © 2012 F. Richmond and B. Mooney, The Center for Applied Management Practices. Modified, from material © 1997- 2011, The Center for Applied Management Practices. Camp Hill, PA 717-730-3705, www.appliedmgt.com.

History, Purpose, and Perspective

1964 – The Beginning

Congress passed the **Economic Opportunity Act** establishing and funding Community Action Agencies and Programs.

1970 – The Mission and the Model

The issuance of **OEO Instruction 6320-1** established the <u>mission</u> and the <u>model</u> (family, agency, and community) of Community Action:

"To stimulate a better focusing of all available local, state, private, and Federal resources upon the goal of enabling *low-income families,* and *low-income individuals* of all ages in rural and urban areas, to attain the skills, knowledge, and motivations and secure the opportunities needed for them to *become self-sufficient."* <u>Family</u>

"The Act thus gives the CAA a primarily catalytic mission: to make the *entire community* more responsive to the needs and interests of the poor by *mobilizing resources* and bringing about greater institutional sensitivity. A CAA's *effectiveness,* therefore, *is measured* not only by the services which it directly provides but, more importantly, *by the improvements and changes it achieves in the community's attitudes and practices toward the poor and in the allocation and focusing of public and private resources for antipoverty purposes."* <u>Community</u>

"In developing its strategy and plans, *the CAA shall take into account the area of greatest community need, the availability of resources,* and its own strengths and limitations. *It should establish realistic, attainable objectives, consistent with the basic mission established in this Instruction, and expressed in concrete terms which permit the measurement of results.* Given the size of the poverty problem and its own limited resources, the CAA should concentrate its efforts on one or two major objectives where it can have the greatest impact." <u>Agency</u>

> Note: this instruction memo was signed by Donald Rumsfeld, then Director of the Office of Economic Opportunity

Participant Manual, "Introduction to ROMA" Version 5.0 © 2012 F. Richmond and B. Mooney, The Center for Applied Management Practices. Modified, from material © 1997- 2011, The Center for Applied Management Practices. Camp Hill, PA 717-730-3705, www.appliedmgt.com.

1974 – What's In a Name?

The Economic Opportunity Act was terminated in 1973, and replaced with the **Community Service Act of 1974**.

The change of name may have given an erroneous signal to the local CAAs who did not study the funding legislation. While the name of the legislation was changed (from "Opportunity" to "Service"), the mission and purpose of the funding remained **unchanged.** Also the direct "Federal-to-local" relationship was preserved.

1981 – The Block Grant
A Change of Relationship

The Community Service Act was replaced by the **Community Service Block Grant (CSBG) Act of 1981.** This changed the regulatory and funding basis of Community Action Agencies and it changed the relationship between local agencies and the Federal government.

State offices were now installed as recipients of the Block Grant funding and therefore as intermediaries for local Community Action Agencies. States were given responsibilities for submitting "community action plans" to identify how funding would be distributed to local agencies, and for assuring that the local agencies were meeting identified community anti-poverty needs.

While the relationship changed with this legislation, the mission and purpose of the legislation did **not change**.

Participant Manual, "Introduction to ROMA" Version 5.0 © 2012 F. Richmond and B. Mooney, The Center for Applied Management Practices. Modified, from material © 1997- 2011, The Center for Applied Management Practices. Camp Hill, PA 717-730-3705, www.appliedmgt.com.

1993 – Measurement and Accountability

Congress passed the **Government Performance and Results Act (GPRA)** in response to a renewed emphasis on accountability.

"The purposes of this Act are to – improve Federal program effectiveness and public accountability by promoting a new focus on results, service quality, and customer satisfaction … and to help Federal managers improve service delivery, by requiring that they plan for meeting program objectives and by providing them with information about program results and service quality."

These points were made regarding the expectations of the Act:

- Establish <u>performance goals</u> to define the level of performance to be achieved by a program activity.
- Express such goals in an <u>objective, quantifiable</u>, and <u>measurable</u> form.
- Describe the <u>operational processes</u>, <u>skills</u>, <u>technology</u>, and the <u>human capital</u>, <u>information</u>, or <u>other resources</u> required to meet the performance goals.
- Establish <u>performance indicators</u> to be used in measuring or assessing the relevant outputs, service levels, and outcomes of each program activity.
- Provide a basis for <u>comparing</u> the actual program results with the established performance goals.
- Describe the means to be used to <u>verify and validate</u> measured values.

Participant Manual, "Introduction to ROMA" Version 5.0 © 2012 F. Richmond and B. Mooney, The Center for Applied Management Practices. Modified, from material © 1997- 2011, The Center for Applied Management Practices. Camp Hill, PA 717-730-3705, www.appliedmgt.com.

1994 – Six National Goals

The 1994 Amendment to the CSBG Act, in response to GPRA, specifically mentioned a requirement for CSBG eligible entities to provide <u>outcome measures</u> to monitor success in three areas: promoting <u>self-sufficiency</u>, <u>family stability</u>, and <u>community revitalization</u>.

In August of 1994, Don Sykes, then director of the Office of Community Services (OCS), created the Monitoring and Assessment Task Force (MATF). The MATF was established to increase the focus of the CSBG Network on performance and results issues as they relate to the work of assisting low-income people. The MATF produced several products, including a National Strategic Plan and the Six National Goals **for community action that specifically addressed the three areas** identified in the '94 amendment, **and added agency goals.**

Goal 1. Low-income people become more self-sufficient. **(Family)**

Goal 2. The conditions in which low-income people live are improved. **(Community)**

Goal 3. Low-income people own a stake in their community. **(Community)**

Goal 4. Partnerships among supporters and providers of services to low-income people are achieved. **(Agency)**

Goal 5. Agencies increase their capacity to achieve results. **(Agency)**

Goal 6. Low-income people, especially vulnerable populations, achieve their potential by strengthening family and other supportive systems. **(Family)**

Participant Manual, "Introduction to ROMA" Version 5.0 © 2012 F. Richmond and B. Mooney, The Center for Applied Management Practices. Modified, from material © 1997- 2011, The Center for Applied Management Practices. Camp Hill, PA 717-730-3705, www.appliedmgt.com.

1994 – Introduction of ROMA

The Monitoring and Assessment Task Force (MATF) advised the Office of Community Services (OCS) to support the <u>development of</u> <u>its own management and accountability practices</u>.

MATF recommended a system to be known as "Results-Oriented Management and Accountability," or <u>ROMA.</u>

ROMA was defined as "a performance-based initiative designed to preserve the anti-poverty focus of community action and to promote greater effectiveness among state and local agencies receiving Community Services Block Grant (CSBG) funds."

Beginning in 1994, ROMA provided a "framework for continuous growth and improvement among more than 1,000 local community action agencies and a basis for state leadership and assistance toward those ends." OCS provided a number of tools and training programs to help individuals in the network increase their understanding of ROMA.

(See <u>www.ROMA1.org</u> for more information.)

At this time, ROMA implementation was voluntary.

In his 1994 "Testimony on Reauthorization of the Community Block Grant Program," Don Sykes, Director of the Office of Community Services (OCS) identified <u>the ROMA approach</u> as a way "to help agencies identify cost effective strategies for reducing gaps in services, improve the capacity of CAAs to partner with innovative community and neighborhood-based initiatives, and help communities better understand the agency's goals and achievements. Timetables for experiencing success from ROMA, which is voluntary, will vary from community to community."

Participant Manual, "Introduction to ROMA" Version 5.0 © 2012 F. Richmond and B. Mooney, The Center for Applied Management Practices. Modified, from material © 1997- 2011, The Center for Applied Management Practices. Camp Hill, PA 717-730-3705, www.appliedmgt.com.

1996 – ROMA Applied in the Network

According to OCS guidance from 1996, "ROMA is a framework for marrying traditional management functions with the new focus on accountability. It is the common language for CAAs to use to respond to the Government Performance and Results Act of 1993, which requires that Federally funded programs demonstrate measurable outcomes."

> ROMA incorporates the use of outcomes/results into the administration, management, operation, and evaluation of human services.
>
> Local CAAs were asked to focus on the achievement of outcomes in addition to the traditional counting of clients and units of service.

To stimulate the implementation of ROMA, OCS supported the creation of a "Train the Trainer" program. A series of tools and practices were developed to increase standard understanding of underlying principles and concepts and to help local agencies embrace ROMA, through a network of National Peer-to-Peer (NPtP) Certified ROMA Trainers.

Sample Logic Model created for the NPtP Project*:

Organization: Program: Family ☐ Agency ☐ Community ☐

Problem Statement	Service or Activity	Outcome	Outcome Indicator	Actual Results	Measurement Tool	Data Source	Frequency of Data Collection and Reporting
Identified Problem, Need, Situation	Identify the # of clients to be served or the # of units offered. Identify the timeframe for the project.	General statement of results expected.	Projected # of clients to achieve the outcome and % of clients who are to be served. Identify the timeframe for the outcome.	Actual # of clients achieving the outcome and the number actually served; the % of clients who achieved the outcome. Identify time frame.	What you will use to document the outcome; the evidence you will collect.	Include both the data collection procedure and the personnel responsible.	
(1) Planning	(2) Intervention	(3) Benefit	(4) Performance	(5) Performance	(6) Accountability	(7) Accountability	(8) Accountability
Organization or Program Mission:							

*F. Richmond modified the Logic Model created by Joseph Wholey to meet the needs of the CSBG network.

Participant Manual, "Introduction to ROMA" Version 5.0 © 2012 F. Richmond and B. Mooney, The Center for Applied Management Practices. Modified, from material © 1997- 2011, The Center for Applied Management Practices. Camp Hill, PA 717-730-3705, www.appliedmgt.com.

1998 – Reauthorization of the CSBG Act

Congress enacted the 1998 Reauthorization of the CSBG Act that included language to **mandate implementation of a comprehensive performance-based management system** across the entire Community Services Network. **ROMA was identified as this system.**

The 1998 Reauthorization required outcome reporting from all CAAs and CSBG eligible entities beginning October 1, 2001.

2001 – Direction from OCS for the First Mandatory Report

The Office of Community Services issued **Information Memo (IM) 49** – Program Challenges, Responsibilities and Strategies – FY 2001-2003.

In this IM, State Offices and CSBG Eligible Entities were provided with guidance regarding the implementation of ROMA and core activities to assist them in preparing for mandatory performance reporting.

In addition to identifying Core Activities required of both State recipients of the Block Grant and local Eligible Entities who ultimately receive the funding, Margaret Washnitzer, then Director of the Division of State Assistance in OCS, asserted in IM 49:

"The Six National ROMA Goals reflect a number of important concepts that transcend CSBG as a stand-alone program. The goals convey the unique strengths that the broader concept of Community Action brings to the Nation's anti-poverty efforts."

Participant Manual, "Introduction to ROMA" Version 5.0 © 2012 F. Richmond and B. Mooney, The Center for Applied Management Practices. Modified, from material © 1997- 2011, The Center for Applied Management Practices. Camp Hill, PA 717-730-3705, www.appliedmgt.com.

2001 – Direction from OCS for first Mandatory Report
(Continued)

Washnitzer further identified important elements of results focused management and ROMA implementation:

Focusing our efforts on client, community, and organizational change, not particular programs or services. As such, the goals provide a basis for <u>results-oriented</u> (not process-based or program-specific) plans, activities, and reports.

> - CAAs must not focus on program-based delivery systems, but rather <u>see how programs work together within the agency to promote changes</u> – not just to provide units of service.
> - The effectiveness of CAAs is measured by the <u>positive impact on the client</u>, resulting from participation in one or multiple programs of the CAA.
> - CAAs work to <u>improve their community</u> as well as their own <u>agency management</u> processes.

Understanding the interdependence of clients, communities, and programs.
The goals recognize that client improvements aggregate to, and reinforce, community improvements, and that strong and well-administered programs underpin both.

> - Emphasizes the <u>interdependence</u> of the family, agency, and community levels, whose effectiveness depends on sound agency management.

Recognizing that CSBG does not succeed as an individual program.
The goals presume that Community Action is most successful when <u>activities supported by a number of funding sources</u> are organized around client and community outcomes, both within an agency and with other service providers.

> - Establishes that CAAs work best in <u>partnership</u> with other community based organizations, that CSBG funds are used to <u>leverage</u> other resources, and that <u>all</u> activities and outcomes of a CAA whether funded by CSBG or other sources are reportable.

Participant Manual, "Introduction to ROMA" Version 5.0 © 2012 F. Richmond and B. Mooney, The Center for Applied Management Practices. Modified, from material © 1997- 2011, The Center for Applied Management Practices. Camp Hill, PA 717-730-3705, www.appliedmgt.com.

2005 – Implementation of National Indicators of Community Action Performance

The National Association of State Community Service Programs (NASCSP) has had administrative responsibility for the national data collection effort since 1987. To comply with mandatory reporting of outcomes, beginning in 2001, several states created standardized indicators, based on their own aggregation and analysis of the measures that had been independently developed at the local agency level.

Notable among these were the reporting systems established in New York, Missouri, and Minnesota, and the Pennsylvania Family Agency Community System (FACS) which was adopted by several other states (CT, WV, and FL) and single agencies in other states, such as AL.

These state identified indicators were reviewed by NASCSP, along with a comprehensive analysis of the "literally thousands of different outcomes" submitted by states between 2001 and 2003. The 2004 NASCSP report, stated: To enable greater aggregation and national reporting of the most universal and significant CSBG results among states and local agencies, twelve common categories, or indicators of community action performance, have been identified from Fiscal Year 2001-2003 data.

OCS reviewed the recommendations of NASCSP and established National Indicators of Community Action Performance (also known as the "National Performance Indicators" or NPIs) in May of 2004.

> The **mandatory performance reports** to OCS include National Performance Indicator data as of fiscal year 2005.

Participant Manual, "Introduction to ROMA" Version 5.0 © 2012 F. Richmond and B. Mooney, The Center for Applied Management Practices. Modified, from material © 1997- 2011, The Center for Applied Management Practices. Camp Hill, PA 717-730-3705, www.appliedmgt.com.

2006 – The ROMA Cycle

As a way to make the directives in IM 49 easier to understand, Mooney and Jakopic* developed the ROMA Cycle graphic seen below. It incorporates the Core Activities for Eligible Entities that are outlined in that directive.

The Results Oriented Management and Accountability Cycle

Assessment
Community needs and resources, agency data

Planning
Use agency mission statement and assessment data to identify results and strategies

Evaluation
Analyze data, compare with benchmarks

Implementation
Services and strategies produce results

Achievement of Results
Observe and report progress

Julie Jakopic, Creating the Vision, and Barbara Mooney, Community Action Association of Pennsylvania, created "Planning for Results" in 2006 as a guide for a results oriented planning process. Initially for this document, they developed the ROMA Cycle to help contextualize the planning process within the full range of ROMA activities identified in IM 49.

Participant Manual, "Introduction to ROMA" Version 5.0 © 2012 F. Richmond and B. Mooney, The Center for Applied Management Practices. Modified, from material © 1997- 2011, The Center for Applied Management Practices. Camp Hill, PA 717-730-3705, www.appliedmgt.com.

2009 – The Obama Administration Renewed Focus on Results

In January 2009, OMB issued the Performance Progress Reporting Form *(PPR)* -- a standard, government-wide performance progress reporting format which is used to collect performance information from recipients of Federal funds. The recipient must submit the *PPR* cover page and any of the forms (*PPR A-F*), which the Federal agency requires, as specified in the award terms and conditions. The ROMA Logic Model is included as PPR C.

2011 – A New Strategy for Excellence*

Other key elements of the administration's focus include:
- Emphasis on place-based services to address the causes and impacts of poverty.
- Increased accountability for performance.
- Promotion of evidence-based practices to achieve results.

These have led to a new strategic approach to streamlining the CSBG T/TA resources that will encourage interoperability among them. OCS developed a national plan that includes the following four priority areas:
1. **Performance Management and Data** – OCS will work with national technical assistance partners and State CSBG lead agencies to **build upon the performance management structure developed through the Results Oriented Management and Accountability (ROMA) system** and the current National Performance Indicators (NPI) that are used to assess program performance.
2. Governance and Legal Technical Assistance.
3. Risk Mitigation and Quality Assurance.
4. Centers of Excellence.

* From IM 123, Reorganization of CSBG T/TA Resources

Participant Manual, "Introduction to ROMA" Version 5.0 © 2012 F. Richmond and B. Mooney, The Center for Applied Management Practices. Modified, from material © 1997- 2011, The Center for Applied Management Practices. Camp Hill, PA 717-730-3705, www.appliedmgt.com.

Module Two

Mission and Community Assessment

The Agency's Mission
Understanding Mission Statements
Activity – Reviewing Mission Statements
Activity – Writing Mission Statements
Mission Change or Mission Drift?
Mission Change
Mission Drift

Community Assessment
Needs Assessment
Is It a Family, Agency, or Community Need?
Activity – What are the Community Needs?
Who Are the Customers? What Do They Value?
Gathering Data for Assessments –Two Kinds of Data
Identifying Community Resources
Analyzing the Assessment Data to Identify Agency Priorities

Learning Objectives:
- Participants are introduced to Peter Drucker's management framework as a support for ROMA principles and practices.
- Participants will be able to understand the purpose of a mission statement and identify its elements.
- Participants identify the difference between Family, Agency, or Community Need statements.
- Participants understand that the proper identification of the problem sets the path for the solution.
- Participants recognize that identification of resources is an important part of the assessment process.
- Participants learn the importance of gathering data from multiple sources to assure a comprehensive community assessment.
- Participants are introduced to data analysis and prioritization processes.

Participant Manual, "Introduction to ROMA" Version 5.0 © 2012 F. Richmond and B. Mooney, The Center for Applied Management Practices. Modified, from material © 1997- 2011, The Center for Applied Management Practices. Camp Hill, PA 717-730-3705, www.appliedmgt.com.

The Agency's Mission

In Module One, you learned that the original purposes of Community Action were:

- assisting families and individuals to become self-sufficient,

- mobilizing public and private resources to make the entire community more responsive to the needs and interests of the poor, and

- bringing about greater institutional sensitivity to poverty.

According to Peter Drucker, an acknowledged expert in the management field:

> "Each social sector institution exists to make a distinctive difference in the lives of individuals and in society. Making this difference is the mission – the organization's purpose and very reason for being…. A mission cannot be impersonal, it has to have deep meaning, be something you believe in…." (p.14)

Drucker Question One is, "What is Our Mission?"

The agency mission is a concise description of the agency's purpose.
It is the foundational statement, upon which the agency builds.
It says why the agency is in business.

Page numbers refer to the Drucker Self Assessment Workbook, 1999

The agency mission should include the following components:

- Is the <u>population</u> to be served identified? Does the mission identify low-income or other designation? Is there a geographic target for population?
- Can you tell from the mission statement the types of <u>services</u> that are administered by the organization or its referrals? (As Drucker says "The hospital isn't going to sell shoes and it's not going into education. It's going to take care of the sick." (p.15)
- Are the <u>expected and achieved outcomes</u> clearly stated? Can you tell what will change?
- Is there any identification of <u>relationships</u> with other organizations that show the connections that help further its mission?

Participant Manual, "Introduction to ROMA" Version 5.0 © 2012 F. Richmond and B. Mooney, The Center for Applied Management Practices. Modified, from material © 1997- 2011, The Center for Applied Management Practices. Camp Hill, PA 717-730-3705, www.appliedmgt.com.

Understanding Mission Statements

Think of the mission statement as a "sound bite."

Can the organization's mission be communicated clearly and concisely in a matter of seconds? Can the organization's mission be understood by the general public or your neighbor?

ACTIVITIES:

There are two activities on the following pages that will help you improve your understanding of mission statements.

The four Key Elements are identified below with examples for each. You may think of other examples.

- Population – Low-income, poverty, special needs.

- Services – Social, human, educational, health, or community services.

- Outcomes – Self-sufficiency, independence, well-being, ready-to-learn.

- Relationship – Partnership, collaboration, referral, agreement, contract.

Tips from Drucker:
The effective mission statement is short and sharply focused. It should fit on a T-shirt. (p.15)

We think it should also fit on the back of a business card.

Participant Manual, "Introduction to ROMA" Version 5.0 © 2012 F. Richmond and B. Mooney, The Center for Applied Management Practices. Modified, from material © 1997- 2011, The Center for Applied Management Practices. Camp Hill, PA 717-730-3705, www.appliedmgt.com.

Activity – Reviewing Mission Statements

> **Instructions:** You have been provided sample mission statements from actual Community Action Agencies, State Community Action Associations, and State CSBG Administrative Offices.
>
> Please evaluate to determine if any, some, or all of the elements of a good mission statement (identified on the previous page) are present. If you find missing elements, consider how adding them would strengthen the sample statements.
>
> Use this page to make notes for discussion with the group.

Participant Manual, "Introduction to ROMA" Version 5.0 © 2012 F. Richmond and B. Mooney, The Center for Applied Management Practices. Modified, from material © 1997- 2011, The Center for Applied Management Practices. Camp Hill, PA 717-730-3705, www.appliedmgt.com.

Activity – Writing Mission Statements

Instructions: Practice writing or evaluating a mission statement for your agency or writing one for your specific program.

Don't forget the key elements: Look for references to the <u>population</u> being served, the <u>services</u> they receive, the <u>relationship</u> to the community, and the expected <u>outcomes</u>.

Mission Change or Mission Drift?

The mission statement of the agency or program should be reviewed on a regular basis; for instance as annual strategic planning is being done.

Anytime there are significant changes — which could be economic, demographic, or environmental (natural or man-made disasters) — or when there are changes in the availability of resources, the mission should be reevaluated.

If the agency had a specific objective and it was accomplished, the agency's mission should also be reevaluated.

Caution: You should not change your agency's mission statement without cause. **Remember the mission of the Community Action Network, as guided by legislation, has not changed since its inception in 1964.** It has been reviewed and found to be a strong statement that is as applicable today as it was then.

Consider the difference between proactively <u>changing</u> a mission statement and passively allowing the agency to "<u>drift</u>" from its original purpose.

Participant Manual, "Introduction to ROMA" Version 5.0 © 2012 F. Richmond and B. Mooney, The Center for Applied Management Practices. Modified, from material © 1997- 2011, The Center for Applied Management Practices. Camp Hill, PA 717-730-3705, www.appliedmgt.com.

Mission Change

Mission Change occurs when the organization:
- has done a comprehensive study of current circumstances,
- has identified a need for restatement of the mission or reorientation of the agency to meet new challenges and opportunities, and
- makes a conscious decision to change the agency focus.

To illustrate when it would be appropriate to change a mission statement, let's look at two examples of organizations that have made <u>specific and deliberate changes</u> to their mission statements.

March of Dimes – This is an example of a mission changed because the organization achieved its goal.

The original mission of the March of Dimes was "To eradicate polio."

What Happened? – They succeeded!
The March of Dimes reinvented itself and today its mission is "improved pregnancy outcomes and reduction and elimination of birth defects through education and research."

YWCA – This is an example of a mission changed because the organization expanded its interests to include new elements.

The original mission of the YWCA was "To provide housing, recreation, and a faith-based community center for young women."

What happened? – The organization changed its focus.
The new YWCA mission is: "eliminating racism, empowering women and promoting peace, justice, freedom and dignity for all by providing safe places for women and girls, building strong women leaders, and advocating for women's rights and civil rights in Congress."

Participant Manual, "Introduction to ROMA" Version 5.0 © 2012 F. Richmond and B. Mooney, The Center for Applied Management Practices. Modified, from material © 1997- 2011, The Center for Applied Management Practices. Camp Hill, PA 717-730-3705, www.appliedmgt.com.

Mission Drift

Mission Drift is the phenomenon which occurs when the agency departs from its original purpose and core values to take on a task that is perhaps related, but not directly in support of the mission. In some cases, this is a response to external events, such as available funding for something the organization never did before. In other cases, internal events can lead to mission drift, such as major turnover of staff and or board members.

Sometimes taking new money requires so much additional work, so much attention to new objectives/new populations/new situations, that the new money actually produces a drain on the agency's other programs.

We find Mission Drift when the agency is attempting to do more activities without putting them in context of existing activities. This causes a dilution of organizational energies, which are then spread over more functions than can be adequately served.

When in doubt whether to head off into another direction because a donor suggests it or a foundation grant opens up a new avenue, analyzing the new direction/activities in relationship to the mission statement will help you stay on course.

Remember that the mission is the basis on which every decision in the agency is to be made.

Drucker tells us:
Defining the nonprofit mission is difficult, painful, and risky. But it alone enables you to set goals and objectives and go to work. Unless the mission is explicitly expressed, clearly understood and supported by every member of the agency, the enterprise is at the mercy of events. Decision makers throughout will decide and act on the basis of different, incompatible and conflicting ideas. They will pull in opposing directions without even being aware of their divergence and your performance is what suffers. (p.15)

Participant Manual, "Introduction to ROMA" Version 5.0 © 2012 F. Richmond and B. Mooney, The Center for Applied Management Practices. Modified, from material © 1997- 2011, The Center for Applied Management Practices. Camp Hill, PA 717-730-3705, www.appliedmgt.com.

Community Assessment

The mission statement as we have seen helps to <u>define why an agency is in business</u>. By identifying a mission statement, the agency has acknowledged a perceived need in the community that it wants to work to eliminate. We have seen some very broad statements of outcomes in the mission statement in the previous segment.

These broad statements are not enough to help the agency develop a strategic plan of action. Before moving to establish the activities of the agency, you must be sure that you understand the needs and resources in the community through a comprehensive assessment.

Community Assessment is a systematic process for <u>creating a profile</u> of the needs and resources of a given community or target population.

It is also a way to identify the assumptions and opinions held by members of the community about key issues.

What is a Community?

Most frequently when we think of a "community," we think of a group of individuals who are considered together because of the place in which they live or work – thus a "community of place" or "place-based community." Such a community can be a state, a county or group of counties in a region, a neighborhood, town, or other geographically specific place. We can identify a number of other kinds of communities, including communities of action, circumstance, inquiry, interest, position, practice, and purpose. (for more information see: <u>http://en.wikipedia.org/wiki/Community_of_place</u>)

It is up to the agency to define its community – either by the geographical location for which it receives funding to serve, or by specific portions of that geography with particular needs (e.g., neighborhood with highest number of low-income residents).

Participant Manual, "Introduction to ROMA" Version 5.0 © 2012 F. Richmond and B. Mooney, The Center for Applied Management Practices. Modified, from material © 1997- 2011, The Center for Applied Management Practices. Camp Hill, PA 717-730-3705, www.appliedmgt.com.

Needs Assessment

"Needs assessment" may be thought of as a way to identify the difference between "what exists" and "what should be."

Agencies gather information so that decisions can be made regarding priority needs to address and outcomes that can be achieved. The assessment of community needs forms the link between the agency's mission and the outcomes it will achieve with its services.

What kinds of needs do communities face?

The CSBG work plan framework establishes a list of service categories that may be addressed by the use of CSBG funding.

The categories (or domains) are:

- Employment
- Education
- Income Management
- Housing
- Emergency Services
- Nutrition

- Linkages
- Self Sufficiency
- Health
- Services for Youth
- Services for Senior Citizens

These have been identified as important areas related to the well-being of a community, the individuals and family members that live in the community, and the agencies that serve the community.

It is not sufficient to identify the varying importance of these broad categories in a community, as this does not provide clear identification of the perceived need facing the low-income population to be served.

- Look back at the Six National Goals and remember that these goals represent three levels; Family, Agency, and Community.

- When we think about needs in our communities, we must see them in these three levels as well.

Participant Manual, "Introduction to ROMA" Version 5.0 © 2012 F. Richmond and B. Mooney, The Center for Applied Management Practices. Modified, from material © 1997- 2011, The Center for Applied Management Practices. Camp Hill, PA 717-730-3705, www.appliedmgt.com.

Is It a Family, Agency, or Community Need?

Let's use the following example of different levels of need in the domain of Education:

Perhaps you feel education is an issue in our community because we have a high-school dropout rate that is above the state average.

Is this an issue that you recognize?

→ You could identify this need as: "Individuals do not have high-school diplomas" which is an individual or family level need. (Family)

Or

→ You could identify the impact that the high dropout rate has on the community, and articulate the need in this way: "Our community does not have youth who are prepared to take productive roles as adults." (Community)

Or

→ You could think about the needs of your agency as it considers the issue of school dropout rates. You might say "Our agency has a need for additional resources to establish or expand GED preparation programs for adult customers who have not graduated high school. (Agency)

You will be able to identify other education needs in these three levels related to specific populations such as: pre-school, elementary and secondary school, adult continuing education, vocational and post-secondary education.

Ask yourself: Whose need is it?

Participant Manual, "Introduction to ROMA" Version 5.0 © 2012 F. Richmond and B. Mooney, The Center for Applied Management Practices. Modified, from material © 1997- 2011, The Center for Applied Management Practices. Camp Hill, PA 717-730-3705, www.appliedmgt.com.

Activity – What are the Community Needs?

Clearly identifying the needs in your community will help you understand the outcomes you want to achieve and the appropriate strategies to address the situation.

Instructions: Identify three issues, concerns, barriers, challenges, or other situations facing the clients in your community, and write these below using a couple words or a sentence for each.
Be sure you can identify if it is a family, agency, or community need.

Next: Go back and number the statements (1, 2, and 3) so that they indicate your priority order. When you present to the group, state your #1 priority even if someone else has already chosen it.

Rules:

- <u>You cannot use one word</u> to identify the need, as this will not help you to understand the situation (it is too broad).
- <u>You cannot say "it's all three,"</u> as this is not helpful as you move forward. We recognize that the problems facing our communities are very complex, and probably involve multiple levels. But you are going to have to clarify the elements of the specific problem you have identified so we can all agree on the level of need.

This process is used to determine needs, as well as to identify the magnitude of the needs in the community, according to "experts." It is often called a Key Informant Survey.

Participant Manual, "Introduction to ROMA" Version 5.0 © 2012 F. Richmond and B. Mooney, The Center for Applied Management Practices. Modified, from material © 1997- 2011, The Center for Applied Management Practices. Camp Hill, PA 717-730-3705, www.appliedmgt.com.

Who Are the Customers?
What Do They Value?

As we consider assessing community needs, emphasis should be placed on making decisions and setting priorities based on information gathered from <u>the people likely to be affected by the needs</u>.

<u>Drucker Question Two</u> is, "Who Are Our Customers?"

Drucker identifies two types of customers:

- The primary customers who are the recipients of services and whose lives will be impacted by direct participation.
- The supporting customers who may be funders, policy makers, family members, partners, and others who have input into services.

Both of these customers must be assessed.

Drucker also cautions: "Customers are never static.... The organization that is devoted to results will adapt and change as they do." (p. 24)

<u>Drucker Question Three</u> is, "What Does the Customer Value?"

"The question, 'What do customers value? What satisfies their needs, wants, and aspirations?' is so complicated that it can only be answered by the customers themselves....Nonprofit leaders tend to ... be convinced they are doing the right things and are so committed to their cause that they come to see the institution as an end in itself...rather than asking 'Does it deliver value to our customers?' (p. 32)

"So begin with (your) assumptions and what you believe your customers value. Then you can compare these beliefs with what customers actually are saying, find the differences, and go on to assess your results." (p. 33)

Page numbers refer to the Drucker Self Assessment Workbook, 1999

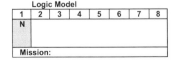

Gathering Data for Assessments
Two Kinds of Data

We have been exploring one kind of data – <u>qualitative data</u> – that you secure from asking someone what they think is important.

- Qualitative data is primarily used when you want to find the depth and breadth of an issue. It provides you with opinions, observations, and other rich, subtle information that you can't get any other way.
- Qualitative data can be characterized as data that is presented in "words." A simple hint is that the "l" in "qual<u>i</u>tative" indicates "letters" or words.

<u>Who</u> would you ask? <u>How</u> would you ask them?

The other kind of data that you need to gather is <u>quantitative data</u> – data that will be used to add a more standardized dimension to the perceptions you have identified.

- Quantitative data provides information in specific categories, such as are collected in "Client Characteristics." This is often referred to as "demographic data." Agency service data can also be useful to identify numbers of customers who have applied, and those impacted by a particular need.
- Quantitative data can be characterized as data that is presented in "numbers." A simple hint is that the "n" in "qua<u>n</u>titative" indicates numbers.

What other kinds of statistical data would you collect that might help you examine the needs of your community?

Participant Manual, "Introduction to ROMA" Version 5.0 © 2012 F. Richmond and B. Mooney, The Center for Applied Management Practices. Modified, from material © 1997- 2011, The Center for Applied Management Practices. Camp Hill, PA 717-730-3705, www.appliedmgt.com.

Identifying Community Resources

When establishing a community profile, it is not sufficient to assess only needs. An important aspect of community assessment is **identifying the resources** that are **currently available** or are **being developed** to address the problems, needs, or situations in the community.

Activity: How do you gather information about these resources?

What about resources that are threatened?

What if your customers don't identify a need because you are filling it with a specific service, and that service is threatened? How do you identify resources that are expected to be lost to the community?

Participant Manual, "Introduction to ROMA" Version 5.0 © 2012 F. Richmond and B. Mooney, The Center for Applied Management Practices. Modified, from material © 1997- 2011, The Center for Applied Management Practices. Camp Hill, PA 717-730-3705, www.appliedmgt.com.

Analyzing the Assessment Data to Identify Agency Priorities

Raw data is not information. It must be analyzed before it becomes useful.

Activity: How does your agency analyze the information from your assessment activities to enable you to move toward the formulation of a plan?

Here are some questions to ask to help organize the information:

- What are some of the root causes of the problem?
- Why should we be interested in the problem?
- What can be done to address the issue?
- Who should address this issue?
- Do we have control, or partial control over this issue?
- Do we have the capabilities to address the issue?
- What programs can address the issue?
- What might we change in our agency that can help address the issue?
- Can we partner with someone to help address the issue?

Participant Manual, "Introduction to ROMA" Version 5.0 © 2012 F. Richmond and B. Mooney, The Center for Applied Management Practices. Modified, from material © 1997- 2011, The Center for Applied Management Practices. Camp Hill, PA 717-730-3705, www.appliedmgt.com.

Analyzing the Assessment Data
to Identify Agency Priorities
(continued)

There are numerous methods to help you identify which issues in your community have risen to the top of the list and ways to help decide which issues the agency will address.

We previously did a quick "prioritization" activity in which we counted up the number of people who agreed that a stated need was the top priority for the agency to address. This is sometimes called a "nominal group process" or a "consensus priority."

A few other techniques available but not presented today are:

- → Identify Root Causes/The Five Whys
- → Force Field Analysis
- → Comparison techniques
- → Cause and effect
- → Trend Analysis

Participant Manual, "Introduction to ROMA" Version 5.0 © 2012 F. Richmond and B. Mooney, The Center for Applied Management Practices. Modified, from material © 1997- 2011, The Center for Applied Management Practices. Camp Hill, PA 717-730-3705, www.appliedmgt.com.

Module Three

Developing Results Oriented Plans

Identifying Outcomes
Activity – Why Plan?
What Comes First?
What Are Our Results?
Assess What Must Be Strengthened or Abandoned
Results or Outcomes?
Types of Outcomes
Examples of Family Outcomes
Examples of Agency Outcomes
Examples of Community Outcomes
Comparison of Family, Agency, and Community Outcomes for Employment
Activity – What Are Our Outcomes?

Identifying Strategies
Connecting Need, Outcomes, and Strategies
Community Action Agencies Are More than Service Providers
Activity – What Are Our Strategies?
Services and Outputs
Activity – Outcomes and Outputs
Proxy Outcomes
Use of Proxy Outcomes

Learning Objectives:
- Participants understand that a Community Action Agency plans for outcomes.
- Participants understand the difference between outcomes and outputs.
- Participants learn the difference between "provision of services" and "strategic thinking" as methods of identifying strategies for their agency.
- Participants understand Proxy Outcomes (outputs that stand in lieu of outcomes).
- Participants understand the importance of selecting strategies and services to be delivered by their agency that match identified community needs, resources, and desired outcomes.

Participant Manual, "Introduction to ROMA" Version 5.0 © 2012 F. Richmond and B. Mooney, The Center for Applied Management Practices. Modified, from material © 1997- 2011, The Center for Applied Management Practices. Camp Hill, PA 717-730-3705, www.appliedmgt.com.

Identifying Outcomes

Why Plan?

> **Instructions:** Think about why planning is part of the ROMA Cycle. Write your ideas below.

Participant Manual, "Introduction to ROMA" Version 5.0 © 2012 F. Richmond and B. Mooney, The Center for Applied Management Practices. Modified, from material © 1997- 2011, The Center for Applied Management Practices. Camp Hill, PA 717-730-3705, www.appliedmgt.com.

What Comes First?

We propose that this is **NOT** the way to seek funding, support, or to allocate resources in your agency.

Rather, you should decide how each funding source (and other resources) can <u>support your mission to meet an identified need.</u>

You also need to consider how all the agency resources <u>support the outcome(s) you wish to achieve.</u>

Participant Manual, "Introduction to ROMA" Version 5.0 © 2012 F. Richmond and B. Mooney, The Center for Applied Management Practices. Modified, from material © 1997- 2011, The Center for Applied Management Practices. Camp Hill, PA 717-730-3705, www.appliedmgt.com.

What Are Our Results?

Drucker advises us that the results of social sector organizations are measured outside the organization in changed lives and changed conditions.

He says that we should look at both "short term accomplishments and long term change." (p. 40)

Drucker Question Four is, "What Are Our Results?"

According to Drucker, "in business you can debate whether profit is really an adequate measuring stick, but without it there is no business in the long term. In the social sector, no such universal standard for success exists. Each organization must identify its customers …and honestly judge whether lives are being changed." (p. 41)

It is up to each agency to identify their successes and assure that they have clear documentation ("evidence") of the success. When these successes are reported to the state CSBG office and to NASCSP, we can begin to understand the common results being achieved across the country.

Data that must be considered during the planning phase of the ROMA Cycle includes agency service data. We must consider the results (or lack of results) that we have achieved in previous years.

Have we been successful?

The answer to this question leads to some hard choices by the agency decision makers.

Page numbers refer to the Drucker Self Assessment Workbook, 1999

Participant Manual, "Introduction to ROMA" Version 5.0 © 2012 F. Richmond and B. Mooney, The Center for Applied Management Practices. Modified, from material © 1997- 2011, The Center for Applied Management Practices. Camp Hill, PA 717-730-3705, www.appliedmgt.com.

Assess What Must Be Strengthened or Abandoned

When we discover that we have not produced results, we must decide if the service should be abandoned or strengthened.

Some things must be abandoned:

"To believe that whatever we do is a moral cause and should be pursued whether there is success or not is a perennial temptation for nonprofit executives — and even more for their boards. Everything is 'a good cause' but we cannot afford to continue where we seem unable to further the mission…

Do we produce results that are sufficiently outstanding for us to justify putting our resources in this area?

Need alone does not justify continuing. Nor does tradition… People in any organization are attached to the obsolete — the things that should have worked but did not, the things that once were productive and no longer are." (p. 43)

However, the agency must be careful to distinguish between programs and services <u>that are not productive</u> and that <u>should no longer be a part of the agency's range of services</u>, and those services that are <u>essential but are currently not producing</u> "outstanding" results.

In the latter case, more resources should be committed to strength the results: **"If essential performance areas are weak, they must be strengthened."** (p. 44)

Page numbers refer to the Drucker Self Assessment Workbook, 1999

What results does the agency want to achieve?

Results or Outcomes? Changes!

We use the word "results" and the word "outcomes" interchangeably as we move through the various principles. Simply put, outcomes or results are changes observed or reported after participation in a service or activity.

For the family, outcomes are changes in knowledge, attitudes, skill or ability, or behavior. For the agency and community, outcomes may be such things as changes in agency or public policy, organizational effectiveness, or social and health conditions.

CAAs and CSBG Eligible Entities, whether private nonprofit community-based organizations or agencies of local government (who provide direct services and/or use subcontractors), produce outcomes for individuals, families, their community, and the agency itself.

Types of Outcomes

Outcomes may happen over time, represent a change in the situation or status, or may be a change in direction for the family, agency, or community.

Change Over Time:
Consider the difference in time frames in different situations. Short-term for a client in need of shelter may be "this afternoon," while short-term for someone obtaining basic job skills training may be six months. You will identify the change to be observed in a time frame that matches the situation. This may be characterized as Short-term, Intermediate-term, or Long-term.

Change in Status:
Situations may be identified at different levels of status. Residents of one public housing project may feel they are safe, while those in another project might feel they are in-crisis, depending on the location, neighbors, and other environmental factors. Some housing situations can be considered thriving.

Change in Direction:
A positive outcome indicates progress toward a goal. A neutral outcome may indicate stability or no change in status. A negative outcome may indicate that the situation has changed for the worst.

Neutral change - maintain status

Participant Manual, "Introduction to ROMA" Version 5.0 © 2012 F. Richmond and B. Mooney, The Center for Applied Management Practices. Modified, from material © 1997- 2011, The Center for Applied Management Practices. Camp Hill, PA 717-730-3705, www.appliedmgt.com.

Examples of Family Outcomes

Low-Income People Become More Self-Sufficient (Goal 1)

Self-sufficiency is <u>more</u> than employment and employment related activities. It can also include outcomes from support activities necessary for the movement towards self-sufficiency and the reduction and elimination of barriers preventing self-sufficiency.

- Unemployed persons obtained employment or self-employment.
- Employed persons obtained better employment or self-employment.
- Persons maintained employment for at least 90 days.
- Persons increased earned income.
- Household resources increased from non-employment sources.
- Persons increased their ability to accumulate and use assets.
- Persons obtained adequate, safe, affordable, unsubsidized, permanent housing.

Low-Income People, Especially Vulnerable Populations, Achieve Their Potential by Strengthening Family and Other Supportive Systems (Goal 6)

There is a broad range of outcomes that are achieved by persons or families who maintain a level of stability or well-being as a result of Community Action.

- Persons increased education or skills.
- Persons increased family functioning skills.
- Persons increased ability to manage income.
- Persons obtained, maintained, or improved housing arrangements.
- Persons reduced or eliminated an emergency need.
- Persons improved or maintained nutrition.
- Persons obtained access to services.
- Persons improved or maintained physical or behavioral health.
- Children and youth achieved expected growth and development.
- Senior citizens and individuals with disabilities maintained independent living.

Participant Manual, "Introduction to ROMA" Version 5.0 © 2012 F. Richmond and B. Mooney, The Center for Applied Management Practices. Modified, from material © 1997- 2011, The Center for Applied Management Practices. Camp Hill, PA 717-730-3705, www.appliedmgt.com.

Examples of Agency Outcomes

Partnerships among Supporters and Providers of Services to Low-Income People are Achieved (Goal 4)

It is not the existence or counting of partnerships and collaborations but the impact these arrangements have on clients and their communities.

- Agencies formed or maintained partnerships and collaborations to coordinate service delivery, improve program efficiency, streamline administration, and/or eliminate the duplication of services.
- Agencies formed or maintained partnerships and collaborations to improve community planning.
- Agencies formed or maintained partnerships and collaborations to achieve specific outcomes.

Agencies Increase Their Capacity to Achieve Results (Goal 5)

Agencies that are well run and meet accepted standards of excellence demonstrate continuous improvement and capacity to meet the needs of low-income individuals/families and communities.

- Agency leveraged external resources (including in-kind and donated) to increase its capacity to serve low-income people.
- Agency maintained sufficient discretionary funding to support unexpected negative cash flow.
- Agency acquired or maintained a common intake system that tracks clients across all agency programs.
- Agency increased ability to document client achievement of outcomes.
- Agency improved implementation of the full range of ROMA activities as identified in the "core activities for eligible entities" in IM 49.
- Agency's Board monitored and improved functioning to support an active tripartite Board as described in IM 82.
- Agency increased or maintained fiscal management that includes adherence to generally accepted accounting practices.
- Agency programs achieved accreditation demonstrating that programs obtained a level of excellence or met or exceeded nationally recognized standards.
- Agency staff obtained credentials that improve their capacity to achieve results.
- Staff and Board participated together in the agency's strategic planning efforts.
- Agency documented increased use of results in agency planning and decision making.

Participant Manual, "Introduction to ROMA" Version 5.0 © 2012 F. Richmond and B. Mooney, The Center for Applied Management Practices. Modified, from material © 1997- 2011, The Center for Applied Management Practices. Camp Hill, PA 717-730-3705, www.appliedmgt.com.

Examples of Community Outcomes

The Conditions in Which Low-Income People Live are Improved (Goal 2)

Community outcomes are an integral part of Community Action and describe the allocation and focusing of public and private resources for antipoverty purposes, improvement in the community infrastructure, and creation of employment and other resources to support low-income people in their transition towards self-sufficiency.

- Low-Income people have improved access to employment, housing, capital, and essential services.
- Municipal infrastructure was maintained or improved.
- The supply of jobs, adequate and affordable housing, community facilities, capital and lending programs, or essential services was increased.
- CAA resources expanded capacity of other agencies to serve low-income people.
- Economic development in the community resulted in employment opportunities for low-income people.
- The scope and number of volunteer opportunities for community participation was created or maintained.

Low-income People Own a Stake in Their Community (Goal 3)

Community outcomes describe the participation of low-income people in community organizations and community activities including volunteer and paid involvement. It includes business and home ownership, indicators of positive community change, and stability.

- The number of low-income persons who participate in formal community organizations, government offices, community boards or councils that provide input to decision-making and reflect the needs of low-income persons was increased or maintained.
- The number and scope of opportunities for low-income persons to participate in advocacy activities resulting in policy and program change was increased or maintained.
- Low-income volunteer participation reduced the need and increased the capacity for agency staff to perform additional functions.
- The number of low-income persons owning businesses was increased.
- The number of low-income persons owning homes was increased.

Participant Manual, "Introduction to ROMA" Version 5.0 © 2012 F. Richmond and B. Mooney, The Center for Applied Management Practices. Modified, from material © 1997- 2011, The Center for Applied Management Practices. Camp Hill, PA 717-730-3705, www.appliedmgt.com.

Comparison of Family, Agency, and Community Outcomes for Employment

Previously we identified <u>needs</u> to be assessed in three levels:
Family, Agency, and Community

Consider the <u>outcomes</u> that are achieved in those same three levels in the Employment domain example below:

> While many social sector organizations help people find employment, CAAs <u>also</u> create jobs, reduce barriers, leverage funds for training, and contribute to the overall economy and economic development of the community.

<u>Family</u> *employment* outcomes can address an individual's employment status such as:
- Secured employment (full, part-time, self employment).
- Improved earnings from income (or received additional benefits).
- Retained employment.

<u>Agency</u> *employment* outcomes can address the relationship of the CAA with other government, community, and private sector organizations to provide additional resources and access to employment:
- Partnership established with public agency for job training and employment placement for low-income people.
- Agreement made with a private corporation for placement of low-income people into employment.

<u>Community</u> *employment* outcomes can address factors that affect the ability to secure and maintain employment:
- New jobs were created in the community.
- Additional public transportation routes (increasing access to jobs for low-income persons) were created.
- Second-shift childcare opportunities for low-income persons were expanded.
- Unemployment rate decreased.

Participant Manual, "Introduction to ROMA" Version 5.0 © 2012 F. Richmond and B. Mooney, The Center for Applied Management Practices. Modified, from material © 1997- 2011, The Center for Applied Management Practices. Camp Hill, PA 717-730-3705, www.appliedmgt.com.

Activity – What Are Our Outcomes?

Instructions: Identify the outcomes your agency can work to achieve. Consider the *needs* identified in Module 2.

Logic Model

1	2	3	4	5	6	7	8
N		O					
Mission:							

Participant Manual, "Introduction to ROMA" Version 5.0 © 2012 F. Richmond and B. Mooney, The Center for Applied Management Practices. Modified, from material © 1997- 2011, The Center for Applied Management Practices. Camp Hill, PA 717-730-3705, www.appliedmgt.com.

Identifying Strategies

Connecting Need, Outcomes, and Strategies

So far, we have seen how the agency's <u>mission statement</u> is the foundation upon which all plans for services must be built. Actions must now be designed to meet specific <u>needs</u> – identified on the family, agency, or community levels. These actions must be designed to meet specific <u>outcomes</u> you plan to achieve, matching the family, agency, or community need.

But what are these actions that the agency will plan to do? We come to the time that the agency must <u>select strategies</u> to achieve the desired outcomes. The strategy can include a service or series of services, advocacy activities, or other actions.

Consider the "plan" developed by this group:

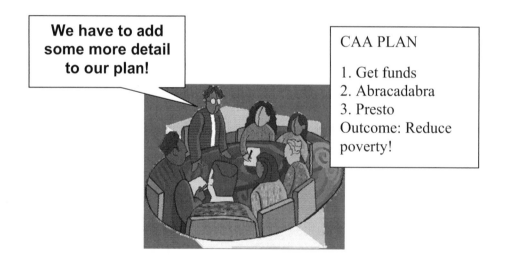

Don't rely on "magic" as a strategy when you make your plan!

You must start with the knowledge of what you want to achieve, identify the resources you have or can bring to the project, and then clearly lay out the services, strategies, advocacy efforts, and other interventions you will implement.

Participant Manual, "Introduction to ROMA" Version 5.0 © 2012 F. Richmond and B. Mooney, The Center for Applied Management Practices. Modified, from material © 1997- 2011, The Center for Applied Management Practices. Camp Hill, PA 717-730-3705, www.appliedmgt.com.

what are pros/cons?

Community Action Agencies Are More than Service Providers

As the agency considers its actions with its available resources targeted to achieving the identified outcomes for its families, communities, or the agency, will it be a "service provider," "self-sufficiency/anti-poverty agent," or both?

PROVISION OF SERVICES MODEL

Agencies that are organized to meet specific short-term services (such as emergency services, transportation, Weatherization) sometimes serve many customers. The <u>challenge</u> is being able to identify <u>long-term change</u> in the customers' lives.

Providing services because funding is available can distract you from a <u>more effective selection</u> of services and strategies.

Failure to link activities together to form a comprehensive set of services and advocacy strategies may <u>reduce your effectiveness</u> in assisting customers to move out of poverty.

Sometimes there are <u>unintended consequences</u> of doing the same services you always have done — *enabling the continuation of poverty.*

STRATEGIC THINKING MODEL

The development of comprehensive strategies must include an understanding of the power of "<u>bundling services</u>" rather than providing services that meet an isolated need.

Agencies must find ways to <u>identify the combination of services</u> that are most effective for helping to change lives and support movement out of poverty.

In addition to providing direct services, agencies must explore the impact of creating <u>community engagement</u> strategies, <u>advocacy</u> and policy change strategies, and other activities that are focused on <u>reduction of poverty</u>.

Agencies must strengthen <u>partnerships</u> to meet the needs that the agency cannot address alone.

Participant Manual, "Introduction to ROMA" Version 5.0 © 2012 F. Richmond and B. Mooney, The Center for Applied Management Practices. Modified, from material © 1997- 2011, The Center for Applied Management Practices. Camp Hill, PA 717-730-3705, www.appliedmgt.com.

Activity – What Are Our Strategies?

Instructions: Consider the needs identified in Module 2 and the outcomes you identified earlier in this module. What activities (services, interventions, advocacy, etc.) can your agency implement to achieve them? Are there things you have been doing that will need to be abandoned in favor of new services? Are there essential services that need strengthened?

Logic Model

1	2	3	4	5	6	7	8
N	S	O					
Mission:							

Participant Manual, "Introduction to ROMA" Version 5.0 © 2012 F. Richmond and B. Mooney, The Center for Applied Management Practices. Modified, from material © 1997- 2011, The Center for Applied Management Practices. Camp Hill, PA 717-730-3705, www.appliedmgt.com.

Services and Outputs

While CAAs are held accountable for producing outcomes, they also must demonstrate they have the capacity to achieve their results through effective and efficient management and delivery of services.

It is clear that when we provide a service, such as a training program, a utility payment, or a ride, this service is not the same as the change that happens to the customer as a result of the service. <u>The changes (the outcomes) are:</u>

- The customer who participates in a training program will increase skills.
- The customer who receives a utility payment will be able to avoid a utility shut off.
- The customer who gets a ride gains access to other services and may therefore have improved health or other observable outcome.

When we talk about the process of the service, the quantity of the work produced by the service or other qualifiers regarding the service, we are talking about "outputs."

Think of other places where the term "output" is used. You hear about the audio or video output of your computer, the artistic output of a painter, or the output of a factory. In these cases, the term can be thought of as the quantity of what is being produced. It can also refer to the production process itself.

Outputs are the activities of the program – both the activities of the provider (the CAA or partners) and the activities of the customers.

Measuring outputs will provide data regarding the scope of the program, but it will not tell you what changes happened to the customers.

Outputs are measured by such things as units of service, number of people served, number of households or families served, amount of service received (hours, dollars, or other measure), hours of participation, or number of times in attendance at a program.

Deciding which elements of the program are outputs and which are outcomes is important for both management and accountability.

On the following page, you will find some examples of various elements of programs typically offered by Community Action Agencies. Please consider if these elements are outcomes or outputs. If you cannot say that something has <u>changed,</u> then the item is probably an output, not an outcome.

The most difficult elements appear to be the ones where customers are participating in a service, which is an output, but staff believe it demonstrates a change, because the customer was not participating before. Think about identifying the customer participation as an output – and the change (the outcome) as something like "improved mastery of soft skills, demonstrated by regular attendance and completion of the training program."

Participant Manual, "Introduction to ROMA" Version 5.0 © 2012 F. Richmond and B. Mooney, The Center for Applied Management Practices. Modified, from material © 1997- 2011, The Center for Applied Management Practices. Camp Hill, PA 717-730-3705, www.appliedmgt.com.

Activity – Outcomes and Outputs

Instructions: The statements below contain both outcomes and outputs for each of the programs. In the space provided, please write the letters "OC" for outcome and the letters "OP" for output.

Adult Basic Education (A.B. E.) Program

_____ Outreach and Recruitment
_____ Enrolls in A.B.E. class
_____ Attends A.B.E. classes
_____ Completes A.B.E. classes (meets attendance requirements)
_____ Achieves competency in basic math, reading, and writing skills
_____ Receives certificate or diploma

Employment Program

_____ Outreach and Recruitment
_____ Enrolls in employability counseling
_____ Completes apprenticeship and masters a skill
_____ Offered employment after successful interview
_____ Obtained part-time employment
_____ Obtained full-time employment
_____ Maintains employment for 90 days

Emergency Assistance

_____ Obtained bag of food
_____ Alleviated hunger
_____ Obtained one month emergency rent payment
_____ Able to stay in apartment
_____ Prevented homelessness
_____ Received check for utility bill
_____ Electric service not shut off
_____ Received a referral to childcare

Weatherization

_____ New furnace installed in home
_____ Homes insulated to R-18
_____ Kitchen appliances repaired or replaced
_____ New thermostat installed
_____ Electric utilization, kkw decreased by 10%
_____ Gas consumption ccf, decreased by 10%
_____ Arrearages eliminated
_____ Energy expenditures reduced
_____ Value of house rises

Conflict Management Program:

_____ Youths are involved in fewer conflicts
_____ Discussion sessions explore experiences with stereotyping, cultural differences
_____ Youth display greater tolerance of differing points of view
_____ Youth practice communication and negotiation skills
_____ Youth report more willingness to have friends with backgrounds different from theirs

After School Program:

_____ Children master new activities
_____ Fifteen (15) at-risk children attend after school sessions
_____ Activities are designed to encourage cooperative play
_____ Children's social skills improve
_____ Children make more positive use of free time outside the program

Parent Education Program:

_____ Parents from 10 families attend workshops
_____ Six group workshops are conducted
_____ Parents' understanding of children's developmental issues increases
_____ Parents provide more age-appropriate guidance to children
_____ Parents participate in role plays and group discussion

Tutoring Program:

_____ Twenty (20) children in grades 4 to 8 are matched with high school tutors
_____ Children's academic performance increases
_____ Children indicate increased belief in their abilities to learn new subjects
_____ Children receive one-to-one help in reading and math
_____ Tutors emphasize the importance of education

Participant Manual, "Introduction to ROMA" Version 5.0 © 2012 F. Richmond and B. Mooney, The Center for Applied Management Practices. Modified, from material © 1997- 2011, The Center for Applied Management Practices. Camp Hill, PA 717-730-3705, www.appliedmgt.com.

Proxy Outcomes
When an Output "Stands In" for an Outcome

In some situations, the receipt of a service is <u>assumed to be the achievement of an outcome.</u>

If a senior citizen receives a <u>home delivered or congregate meal</u> (output), you assume that the person has reduced hunger (outcome) or increased nutrition (outcome).

It would be impractical for you to actually test to assure "reduced hunger" or "increased nutrition" has occurred. Fortunately, <u>there is sufficient research data</u> to support these outcomes for those eligible to participate in congregate or home delivered meal programs. This research determines that a specific group of clients who are at risk of negative behaviors would benefit from the program and achieve some, if not all, of the expected outcomes as described in the supporting research.

Therefore, the <u>count of people receiving meals</u> (NOT the number of meals provided) then becomes a <u>proxy outcome</u> for the real outcome of "reduced hunger."

Research also tells us that there are other outcomes associated with a home delivered meal program. These include: <u>increased safety</u>, <u>decreased isolation and depression</u>, and <u>maintaining independence</u>. It is not practical to expect a home delivered meal program to collect data on the above outcomes. The count of the number of people who received meals can become a proxy for outcomes that cannot be realistically measured.

In these cases, where research supports the causative relationship between the service and the outcome, the intervention, activity, or service becomes a proxy outcome, counted "in place of" the actual outcome.

Participant Manual, "Introduction to ROMA" Version 5.0 © 2012 F. Richmond and B. Mooney, The Center for Applied Management Practices. Modified, from material © 1997- 2011, The Center for Applied Management Practices. Camp Hill, PA 717-730-3705, www.appliedmgt.com.

Use of Proxy Outcomes

A proxy outcome is best used when these conditions are present:

- Actual outcome is <u>supported by previous research</u> and it is not practical to measure or collect at each site

- The outcome is <u>recognized and accepted</u> to be related to the service because of established research.

- The client is eligible for the intervention, activity, or service and the research shows that clients <u>with the eligibility requirements</u> who participate <u>will yield the expected outcome</u>(s).

Another Example of a Proxy Outcome – After School Program

- If you provide an after school program that includes a homework helper component, you should be able to identify an <u>improvement in grades</u> for students who attend; or an improvement in school behavior. These would be <u>the measurable outcomes</u> for the program.

- However, research shows that after school programs also impact on the <u>reduction of juvenile crime</u> and the <u>reduction of teen pregnancies</u> (considered to be negative behaviors). These are real outcomes, but local programs cannot document that you prevented something from happening. Therefore, measuring attendance/participation* in these situations is considered an acceptable proxy for the other outcomes.

- The count of the number of students who attended the program could be a proxy for the number of students who reduced negative behavior.

*Identification of attendance or participation as a proxy outcome is not to be routinely accepted or used without proper supporting research.

Participant Manual, "Introduction to ROMA" Version 5.0 © 2012 F. Richmond and B. Mooney, The Center for Applied Management Practices. Modified, from material © 1997- 2011, The Center for Applied Management Practices. Camp Hill, PA 717-730-3705, www.appliedmgt.com.

Module Four

Implementing the Plan

What Is Our Plan?
Implementing the Plan
Reginald Carter's Seven Key Questions
Characteristics of Outcome Indicators
Identifying Outcome Indicators
Examples of Multiple Indicators for an Outcome
Activity – What Are Our Outcome Indicators?
Implementation of National Indicators of Community Action Performance
Beyond National Indicators

Learning Objectives:
- Participants will understand the importance of appraising the plan prior to implementation.
- Participants will be introduced to Reginald Carter and the Seven Key Questions used to support planning and management.
- Participants will be able to identify outcome indicators.
- Participants practice creating outcome indicators for identified needs, outcomes, and strategies.
- Participants are introduced to the standard set of performance indicators established for all CAAs.

Participant Manual, "Introduction to ROMA" Version 5.0 © 2012 F. Richmond and B. Mooney, The Center for Applied Management Practices. Modified, from material © 1997- 2011, The Center for Applied Management Practices. Camp Hill, PA 717-730-3705, www.appliedmgt.com.

What Is Our Plan?

Drucker tells us that the written plan will help us "get the right things done." (p. 52) He also reminds us of the importance of involvement of the agency Board of Directors.

Drucker Question Five is, "What Is Our Plan?"

"The self assessment process leads to a plan that is a concise summation of the organization's purpose and future direction....The development and formal adoption of mission and goals are fundamental to effective governance of a nonprofit organization and are primary responsibilities of the board. Therefore these strategic elements of the plan must be approved by the board." (p. 52)

Page numbers refer to the Drucker Self Assessment Workbook, 1999

In the identification of the core activities for Eligible Entities, IM 49 specifically identifies these activities as the responsibility of "the entity and its board."

The written plan isn't about having strategies and outcomes fixed for all time in a document, but more about proving the ability to continuously refer back to the plan as you move forward. You will review and appraise the value of each element, so you can update it as data is collected and analyzed. The plan must be flexible enough to reflect community changes around you.

"True self-assessment is never finished. Leadership requires that constant resharpening, refocusing, never really being satisfied." (Drucker, p. 56)

According to Information Memorandum 49, the plan should take into account:
- strategies that use existing resources and develop new ones to address needs,
- the relationship of activities supported by the Agency to other anti-poverty, community development services in community, and
- the extent Agency activities contribute to the accomplishment of one or more of the six national ROMA goals.

Implementing the Plan

A well written plan leads to sound agency management and accountability…provided the plan is implemented well.

Drucker cautions us: "Work doesn't get done by a magnificent statement of policy. Work is only done when it is done. Done by people. By people who are properly informed, assigned and equipped." (p. 59)

"The nonprofit organization must be information-based. Information must flow from the individuals doing the work to the board management, and it must flow back as well." (p.59)

"What we measure and how we measure it determines what will be considered relevant and thereby determines not just what we see but what we and others do." (p.60)

The agency's strategic plan guides the implementation of your strategies to achieve results. But before you can implement your plan, you must understand the elements which must be operationalized for quality service delivery. These include:

- identifying the fundamental elements necessary for implementation, and

- identifying procedures and personnel for observation and reporting of results.

We have help from Reginald Carter with some questions to guide us as we consider how we will implement our plan.

Participant Manual, "Introduction to ROMA" Version 5.0 © 2012 F. Richmond and B. Mooney, The Center for Applied Management Practices. Modified, from material © 1997- 2011, The Center for Applied Management Practices. Camp Hill, PA 717-730-3705, www.appliedmgt.com.

Reginald Carter's Seven Key Questions

Dr. Reginald Carter used his experiences as the Director of Planning and Evaluation for the Michigan Department of Social Services as the basis for writing **The Accountable Agency (1983).** [1]

Carter states that each year when a program manager presents a budget for services to be implemented, there are seven questions that should be asked. He proposes that <u>all agencies should be able to answer these seven questions</u> in order to justify the budget amounts that will support the activities of the agency.

You should be able to answer these questions as you begin to implement your plan.

1. How many clients are you serving?
2. Who are they?
3. What services do you give them?
4. What does it cost?
5. What does it cost per service delivered?
6. What happens to the clients as a result of the service?
7. What does it cost per outcome?

These questions also frame criteria for accountability that include both <u>efficiency</u> and <u>effectiveness</u> measures.

> **Note: We will use the shaded questions in the *Introduction to ROMA*, and return to the budget and cost questions** (4, 5, and 7) **in later sessions.**

---

[1] © The <u>Accountable Agency</u>, Reginald Carter, Sage Human Services Guide 34, 1983. **This book is available free, downloaded at: <u>www.appliedmgt.com</u>.**

Participant Manual, "Introduction to ROMA" Version 5.0 © 2012 F. Richmond and B. Mooney, The Center for Applied Management Practices. Modified, from material © 1997- 2011, The Center for Applied Management Practices. Camp Hill, PA 717-730-3705, www.appliedmgt.com.

Carter's Key Questions - Continued

1. How many clients are you serving?

- **The number of individuals projected to be served is often based on budget and other resource data. This projected number is important as you implement your plan.**

- **Agencies must be able to provide unduplicated counts of their clients being served. Without this ability, <u>clients may be counted multiple times.</u>**

If the agency does not have a common intake <u>or</u> common identification number, and each program or service assigns their own identification number, the agency will in all likelihood have a duplicated client count. This is also known as a silo or smokestack approach.

To assure an unduplicated count, each person/family is considered to be a <u>client of the agency</u> and not an individual program. In this method, they are <u>assigned a single identification number, which would go along with the client to any program or service received.</u>

- **There are other factors that will affect how the agency counts clients. The agency must determine when a person/family becomes a client, which may vary by program. Lack of standardization may result in an <u>undercount of clients</u>.**

Does receipt of any type of service, qualify an individual as a client? For example, if the service is for information only or a brief referral, is the person a client of the Information and Referral service of the agency? How is this individual counted?

2. Who are they?

- **In the plan, the agency may have identified a specific target population, based on the community assessment.**

- **Upon intake and assessment, the agency must collect basic demographic and characteristic data such as age, gender, income, employment, education, disability level, race, and ethnicity.**

- **This data can clarify the outcome information.**

For example, information about clients could help you understand the elements that make a difference in one's ability to find and maintain a job. Is it a prior work history? Could it be age, race, gender, neighborhood, or other factors that affects the successful outcome?

Participant Manual, "Introduction to ROMA" Version 5.0 © 2012 F. Richmond and B. Mooney, The Center for Applied Management Practices. Modified, from material © 1997- 2011, The Center for Applied Management Practices. Camp Hill, PA 717-730-3705, www.appliedmgt.com.

Carter's Key Questions - Continued

3. What service(s) do you give them?

Agencies must:

- Determine which clients received which service(s) resulting in a specific outcome.

- Identify how many services are offered (count) and how often services are offered (frequency).

- Be able to recognize and assess the quality of the services offered.

It is important to <u>determine the relationship between the service and the expected outcome. This is key in the evaluation of the effectiveness of the program</u> in producing desired results. Without this information, you cannot determine if the program should be expanded, reduced, or maintained.

6. What happens to the clients as a result of the service?

- Identify the <u>outcome(s)</u> to be achieved by the client's participation in the service.

- Identify the number of clients who are <u>projected to achieve</u> the outcome and the number of clients who <u>actually achieved</u> the outcome.
- If there is only one service provided, it is easy to link it to an expected outcome or result. <u>It is more difficult to assign or link expected outcomes where multiple services are provided.</u>

There are four possible relationships between provision of services and expected outcomes:
  - One Service: One Outcome
  - One Service: Multiple Outcomes
  - Multiple Services: One Outcome
  - Multiple Services: Multiple Outcomes

Participant Manual, "Introduction to ROMA" Version 5.0 © 2012 F. Richmond and B. Mooney, The Center for Applied Management Practices. Modified, from material © 1997- 2011, The Center for Applied Management Practices. Camp Hill, PA 717-730-3705, www.appliedmgt.com.

Characteristics of Outcome Indicators

In our Logic Model, outcomes are statements of results without numbers. If we are to identify "what happens," we need to be able to also define the scope of the outcomes by establishing outcome indicators.

When you start adding numbers, you move from <u>outcome statements</u> to <u>outcome indicator statements</u>.

The <u>outcome statement</u> is a general statement of change without numbers, and the <u>indicator</u> is the statement of <u>how much</u> something has changed or <u>how many</u> have changed.

The indicator contains specific information about the scope of success. How many people changed? How much change was observed? How well was the outcome achieved?

Outcome Indicators meet all of these characteristics:
☐ Measurable.
☐ Simple, clear, and understandable.
☐ Realistic or attainable.
☐ Manageable.
☐ Identifies a specific client or group of clients.
☐ Specifies a time frame.
☐ Measures an end, not a means to an end.

Some people refer to the mnemonic word, <u>SMART</u>, as a way to remember the elements of a good indicator — which covers most of the elements listed above:
- <u>S</u>pecific (clear, understandable)
- <u>M</u>easurable
- <u>A</u>ttainable (realistic)
- <u>R</u>elevant (to the specific client or group)
- <u>T</u>ime specific

Participant Manual, "Introduction to ROMA" Version 5.0 © 2012 F. Richmond and B. Mooney, The Center for Applied Management Practices. Modified, from material © 1997- 2011, The Center for Applied Management Practices. Camp Hill, PA 717-730-3705, www.appliedmgt.com.

Identifying Outcome Indicators

In the examples below, the outcome indicators identify what is observed and what can be measured to verify that a change was achieved.

Note: A clearly stated indicator will help you define what data will be collected as evidence that the outcome you expect has been achieved.

The outcome "<u>school success</u>" is too broad to allow you to measure it. You must decide what "indicates" school success.
Some ideas are:

- Improved grades *(which you could measure by a report card)*
- Reduced absences *(data also on report cards)*
- Improved behavior *(data to be collected by teacher observation)*

An indicator of "<u>improved use of the English language</u>" may include a specific improvement in the use of English, which could be measured -- for example by scores on the Basic English Skills Test *(BEST),* a standardized test used in English as a Second Language programs.

An indicator of "<u>increased family functioning</u>" may include specific behavior changes, which could be measured, for example, by scores on the Global Assessment Functioning Scale *(GAF), a standardized scale that is used in the mental health field that helps determine the level of functioning of an individual who is in care.*

Identifying the indicator requires even more specificity than what we have above. We need to quantify our expectations:

- How many students will improve?
- What is the expected improvement (by how much)?
- How many absences are acceptable?
- How will you quantify the improved behavior?

The indicator will include the <u>number of clients who are expected to achieve the specifically defined "change" or outcome</u> in relationship to the <u>number who will receive service</u>. It will often include a <u>time frame</u>.

Participant Manual, "Introduction to ROMA" Version 5.0 © 2012 F. Richmond and B. Mooney, The Center for Applied Management Practices. Modified, from material © 1997- 2011, The Center for Applied Management Practices. Camp Hill, PA 717-730-3705, www.appliedmgt.com.

Examples of Multiple Indicators for an Outcome

Example 1 – In some cases, the outcomes achieved by recipients of service may fall along a continuum.

The <u>outcome</u> of <u>employment and training services to 50 clients</u> is "obtaining a job." The primary indicator is:

- 10/50 clients obtain full-time jobs above minimum wage, including benefits, and are employed 90 days after placement.

Other indicators could include:

- 20/50 obtain permanent full-time jobs at minimum wage without benefits and are employed 90 days after placement;
- 10/50 obtain part-time temporary jobs;
- 5/50 improve skills and experience through on-the-job training programs;
- 5/50 remain unemployed after 180 days in the program.

Example 2 – In other cases (e.g., when referrals to other services may be involved), there may be multiple outcome indicators that cross a number of domains.

The <u>outcome</u> of providing <u>case management services to 20 families</u> could be "self sufficiency." The range of <u>indicators</u> could include:

- 3/20 families increased their household income by 20% or more from all income sources;
- 1/20 persons opened a home-based childcare center (became self employed);
- 5/20 families obtained safe, affordable rental housing;
- 1/20 families purchased a home;
- 3/20 persons achieved G.E.D. high-school equivalency diploma;
- 1/20 persons increased basic academic skills;
- 1/20 persons increased English language skills;
- 5/20 families continue to receive case management services but have not achieved any goal on their case management plan.

Note: In this example, each person achieved a different outcome, but in reality, one person could have achieved two or three of these outcomes.

Participant Manual, "Introduction to ROMA" Version 5.0 © 2012 F. Richmond and B. Mooney, The Center for Applied Management Practices. Modified, from material © 1997- 2011, The Center for Applied Management Practices. Camp Hill, PA 717-730-3705, www.appliedmgt.com.

Activity – What Are Our Outcome Indicators?

<u>Instructions:</u> Consider the needs identified in Module 2 and the outcomes and strategies you identified in Module 3. How can you refine the outcomes to include projected targets, identified indicators, and time frame?

Use this formula:

_____(a) out of _____(b) will achieve the outcome (as you plan to measure it) within this time frame: _____(c)

- (a)   Projection of the number of persons expected to achieve the outcome. This is the numerator.
- (b)   The total number of persons receiving the service. This is the denominator.
- (c)   The time frame.

For example: <u>10</u> out of <u>50</u> persons in the employment program will obtain a job, <u>six months</u> after enrollment.

Logic Model							
1	2	3	4	5	6	7	8
N	S	O	OI				
Mission:							

Participant Manual, "Introduction to ROMA" Version 5.0 © 2012 F. Richmond and B. Mooney, The Center for Applied Management Practices. Modified, from material © 1997- 2011, The Center for Applied Management Practices. Camp Hill, PA 717-730-3705, www.appliedmgt.com.

Implementation of National Indicators of Community Action Performance

As we have seen in Module One (History), the first mandated report of Community Action performance results was in 2001.

The results reported between 2001 and 2003 were analyzed to produce a more standardized format to guide the reporting of community action outcomes. Efforts like those that produced the Pennsylvania FACS Report in 1998 and other state wide systems across were also reviewed by NASCSP and the OCS Information System Task Force (ISTF).

See http://www.roma-nptp.org/resources.html for more information about the ISTF.

From the 2003 NASCSP report: The Community Services Network is moving to <u>balance the localized nature of its work and outcomes with the need to create a more uniform and accurate national accounting</u> of how community action improves conditions and opportunities for low-income families and their communities.

In 2004, fifteen (15) national performance indicators (NPIs)* were created collaboratively within the Community Services Network to enable approximately 1,000 diverse Community Action Agencies in all 50 states and territories to present a more uniform and coherent national picture of their work and accomplishments.

Reporting of national performance indicators is an important component of the broader community action initiative to use results-focused management principles to revitalize and strengthen the entire Community Services Network.

<u>The National Performance Indicators (NPIs) are about Community Action, not just the Community Services Block Grant.</u> Outcomes should be counted and reported from all relevant community action programs and activities.

Excerpt from the "Guide to the National Indicators of Community Action Performance," Issued by NASCSP in 2004.

Each National Indicator is followed by sub-indicators. There were 92 indicators and sub-indicators and a section of items which are service counts (6.5) in the original set of NPIs.

See www.nascsp.org for the current set of NPIs.

Participant Manual, "Introduction to ROMA" Version 5.0 © 2012 F. Richmond and B. Mooney, The Center for Applied Management Practices. Modified, from material © 1997- 2011, The Center for Applied Management Practices. Camp Hill, PA 717-730-3705, www.appliedmgt.com.

Beyond National Performance Indicators

It is important to recognize that while the NPIs have provided a standardized way to think about the results of Community Action services, the set of indicators and sub-indicators is not complete.

When the NPIs became the basis of the performance portion of the Information System (IS) Report, it was acknowledged that by focusing on the most commonly identified outcomes, other outcomes would not be reported under the NPIs.

The National Performance Indicators reflect only a portion of the work and accomplishments of Community Action. This is not our complete story, but a selective sampling of what we do.

"Because of the nature of the Community Services Block Grant, agencies participate in a broad range of activities to meet the unique needs of their communities. Each agency captures outcome data specific to its unique goals and priorities. It should be noted that not all agencies participate in the activities that generate outcomes for every national indicator, nor do these indicators represent all of the outcomes achieved by agencies."

"Guide to the National Indicators of Community Action Performance,"
NASCSP, 2004

Community Action Agencies are encouraged to continue to report annually on their full range of outcomes in addition to reporting on the required national indicators.

There are blank lines following each of the standard indicators where agencies are invited to include additional indicators.

Indicators and sub-indicators are changed in response to additional indicators provided from the field, to capture outcomes related to some major focus (such as ARRA) or to meet other network needs.

Changes to the NPIs are made periodically, based on the input of the Information Systems Task Force (ISTF).

Participant Manual, "Introduction to ROMA" Version 5.0 © 2012 F. Richmond and B. Mooney, The Center for Applied Management Practices. Modified, from material © 1997- 2011, The Center for Applied Management Practices. Camp Hill, PA 717-730-3705, www.appliedmgt.com.

Module Five

Measuring Performance and Establishing Standards

Using Carter's Seven Key Questions for Performance and Accountability
Establishing Targets and Measuring Performance
Establishing Targets and Measuring Performance – An Example
Measuring Actual Performance With a Reduced Denominator
Activity – What is Our Projected Success Rate?
Establishing Performance Standards
Activity – Let's Talk Baseball!
Activity – Success Measures in Industry
What Can We Learn From Baseball?
Activity – Success Measures in Industry
Performance Targeting for NPIs – Another Way to Calculate Success
Another Dimension of Performance
Establishing Measurement Tools and Processes
Identifying Evidence
Activity – What Are Our Measurement Tools and Processes?

Learning Objectives:

- Participants will understand how to use data from the Carter Questions to identify performance and accountability.
- Participants will learn to identify how to calculate success for the CSBG network in two ways.
- Participants will learn what baseball teaches us about measuring performance.
- Participants will identify industry standards for performance.
- Participants will identify measurement tools and processes.
- Participants practice matching outcomes and indicators to measurement tools and processes.

Participant Manual, "Introduction to ROMA" Version 5.0 © 2012 F. Richmond and B. Mooney, The Center for Applied Management Practices. Modified, from material © 1997- 2011, The Center for Applied Management Practices. Camp Hill, PA 717-730-3705, www.appliedmgt.com.

Using Carter's Seven Key Questions for Performance and Accountability

We identified the Carter Questions in Module 4, and showed how they could be used in planning and management.

Now we need to think about using Questions 1, 3, and 6 as a basis for calculating performance and establishing accountability measures.

1. How many clients are you serving?

3. What services do you give them?

6. What happens to the clients as a result of the service?

The next addition to our logic model is a calculation that will produce a <u>measure of performance</u>.

**We saw in the creation of the indicator that we establish a relationship between the number of clients who were served and the number of clients who achieved results.
Such as: 10 out of 50 got a job.
This is the basis for the calculation that follows.**

Participant Manual, "Introduction to ROMA" Version 5.0 © 2012 F. Richmond and B. Mooney, The Center for Applied Management Practices. Modified, from material © 1997- 2011, The Center for Applied Management Practices. Camp Hill, PA 717-730-3705, www.appliedmgt.com.

Establishing Targets and Measuring Performance

There are five steps used to identify <u>expected performance</u> and a final sixth step to determine <u>actual performance</u>.

1. **<u>Identify the outcome(s).</u>** This is a qualitative statement about what is going to be achieved, **with no numbers**. (Carter Question 6)

2. **<u>Identify the service</u>, activity, intervention, or output that is expected to produce the outcome.** (Carter Question 3)

3. **<u>Identify the number of people receiving the service</u>.** (Carter Question 1) Identify a timeframe as a part of the description of the service.

4. **<u>Identify the outcome indicator(s)</u>.** This is a **quantitative statement** where the number of <u>clients or units that are expected to achieve the outcome</u> is added to the general outcome statement.

5. **<u>Estimate performance</u>** by calculating the relationship between the number receiving the service and the number achieving the outcome. Divide the number expected to achieve the outcome (placed in the numerator of a fraction you are creating) by the number expected to receive the service (placed in the denominator of the fraction) to get a percent. This calculation yields a percentage which is the "projected success rate."

<u>**These steps occur prior to delivery of the service**</u> and are used to target, or estimate, your performance for the service.

<u>**The final step occurs after the service,**</u> when you know what happened, to determine your "actual success rate".

6. **<u>Actual performance is calculated</u>** after delivery of the service using the same process as above but replacing the projected or targeted numbers with the actual numbers <u>in both the numerator and the denominator</u>.

The analysis of performance will include comparing the projected success rate percentage with the actual success rate percentage.

Logic Model

1	2	3	4	5	6	7	8
N	S	O	OI	R			

Mission:

Participant Manual, "Introduction to ROMA" Version 5.0 © 2012 F. Richmond and B. Mooney, The Center for Applied Management Practices. Modified, from material © 1997- 2011, The Center for Applied Management Practices. Camp Hill, PA 717-730-3705, www.appliedmgt.com.

Establishing Targets and Measuring Performance – An Example

Estimating Performance:

A family self-sufficiency program has enrolled <u>20 families (D)</u> who will receive case management services over the next six months. It is estimated or projected that <u>seven of the families (N)</u> will increase their household income as a result of various activities coordinated by the case manager.

1. <u>Outcome</u> – Increase household income.
2. <u>Service/Activity</u>– Case-managed family self-sufficiency program.
3. <u>Number to be served (D)</u> – 20 families in a six-month period.
4. <u>Outcome Indicator (N)</u> – 7 families will increase household income by 10% in six months.
5. <u>Projected success rate</u> – 7 families who will have achieved the outcome divided by 20 families receiving services = 35% will succeed.

$$\frac{\text{(N) 7 families increase household income}}{\text{(D) 20 families enrolled in case management}} = 35\% \textbf{ projected success rate}$$

Measuring Actual Performance:

- After the service had been provided, the program identified the <u>actual</u> number of clients who achieved the outcome within the established timeframe and calculated the success rate. <u>This requires follow-up</u>.
- This number was <u>5 families</u>.
- Five (5) families achieved the outcome divided by 20 families receiving services = 25% actually succeeded.

$$\frac{\text{(N) 5 families increased household income}}{\text{(D) 20 families enrolled in case management}} = 25\% \textbf{ actual success rate}$$

Participant Manual, "Introduction to ROMA" Version 5.0 © 2012 F. Richmond and B. Mooney, The Center for Applied Management Practices. Modified, from material © 1997- 2011, The Center for Applied Management Practices. Camp Hill, PA 717-730-3705, www.appliedmgt.com.

Measuring Actual Performance
With a Reduced Denominator

If you are managing your program using results-oriented practices, you will want to know how many individuals you will need to serve to achieve certain goals. Let's assume that some individuals who enroll will not complete the program.

How does this drop-out affect your performance rate?

For example, if of the 20 families enrolled in the case management, you find that at the end of the program 15 families complete all requirements, do you use the 20 as the denominator or base or do you use 15?

We saw previously that the actual performance rate for this program is 25% (5/20). If the CAA only counts those completing the program (15), it inflates the success rate from 25% to 33%.

$$\frac{\text{5 families increase household income}}{\text{15 families } \textit{completed requirements}} = 33\% \text{ success rate for those families who completed}$$

(15 of the 20 who enrolled)

Accountability and need for data that support allocation of resources require documentation of all people served. Therefore, it is helpful to management to calculate both measures of performance, comparing the percent that represents all the original enrollments (25% success), with the percent that represents those that completed the program (33% success). In this way, you can identify the success for the "completers" which is a measure of the effectiveness of the service and also account for all who received service.

- What this might mean is that you will need to recruit additional individuals to enroll in order to reach the number who will complete if you want to achieve the number of successes you project.
- Another situation when you might use a reduced denominator is when the actual number of participants served was less than projected.
- Similarly, if the actual number was higher than projected, the denominator would reflect an increased denominator.
- Always use the actual numbers in the follow-up calculations.

Participant Manual, "Introduction to ROMA" Version 5.0 © 2012 F. Richmond and B. Mooney, The Center for Applied Management Practices. Modified, from material © 1997- 2011, The Center for Applied Management Practices. Camp Hill, PA 717-730-3705, www.appliedmgt.com.

Activity – What Is Our Projected Success Rate?

Instructions: Include the calculation for the percent of success from the information identified in the previous module.

_____(a) out of _____(b) or _____% (a/b) will (achieve the outcome) within the time frame: _____(c)

(a)   Projection of the number of persons expected to achieve the outcome. This is the numerator.

(b)   Projection of the total number of persons to receive the service. This is the denominator.

(a/b)   Divide the number who achieved the outcome by the number receiving the service. This is the projected success rate.

(c)   The time frame for this measurement.

For example: 10 out of 20 persons in the employment program or 50% obtained a job six months after enrollment.

Note: Amend the information you previously entered into the Outcome Indicator column of the logic model.

Once the service is complete, you will convert this statement by using (a) the number that actually achieved, (b) the number actually served, and the calculation of the percent of success.

Is your percent "Good"? What is the standard?

Participant Manual, "Introduction to ROMA" Version 5.0 © 2012 F. Richmond and B. Mooney, The Center for Applied Management Practices. Modified, from material © 1997- 2011, The Center for Applied Management Practices. Camp Hill, PA 717-730-3705, www.appliedmgt.com.

Establishing Performance Standards

How do you know what percent of success is realistic or achievable?

Activity – Let's Talk Baseball!

Instructions: You will receive a baseball card, which will be for a <u>batter</u> rather than a <u>pitcher</u>. On the back of the card is a <u>batting average</u>. Please write the batting average below. The batting average is a three-digit number beginning with a decimal point, e.g., <u>.273</u>. This is the statistic that is used to measure a batter's performance.

Write the batting average here:

Participant Manual, "Introduction to ROMA" Version 5.0 © 2012 F. Richmond and B. Mooney, The Center for Applied Management Practices. Modified, from material © 1997- 2011, The Center for Applied Management Practices. Camp Hill, PA 717-730-3705, www.appliedmgt.com.

Activity – Let's Talk Baseball! - Continued

In baseball, while we collect the number of times a player is "at bat," (attendance or participation), what baseball wants to know is the result of being "at bat." Did the player officially get up to bat and get a hit? This result or outcome indicator is a performance calculation called the batting average.

We illustrate with Yogi Berra's baseball card.

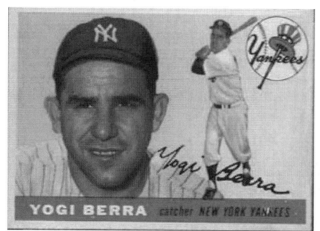 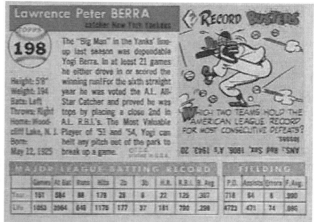

N= <u>179 hits</u>   = .307 batting average
D=   584 times at bat

Yogi Berra successfully hit the ball and got on base 30.7% of the time. In baseball, a batting average:

- at .300 (30%) or greater is a superstar,
- between .299-.250 (29.9%-25%) is achieved by the majority of players,
- equal to or less than .249 (24.9%) is achieved by the least successful ball players.

Yogi Berra was a superstar, but unless baseball "taught" us that 30% was highly successful, we may have thought of him as a failure.

Participant Manual, "Introduction to ROMA" Version 5.0 © 2012 F. Richmond and B. Mooney, The Center for Applied Management Practices. Modified, from material © 1997- 2011, The Center for Applied Management Practices. Camp Hill, PA 717-730-3705, www.appliedmgt.com.

What Can We Learn From Baseball?

Baseball began collecting statistics before 1876 — and they started with a pencil and paper. In over 136 years, baseball has <u>developed standards of performance</u>.

Hitting .300, or succeeding about 30% of the time, is a recognized and accepted measure of excellence. The ball player who achieves this is a superstar. But if baseball had not discovered the relationship between the hitting standard and winning games, through collection and analysis of data, we would not know that we are <u>observing success</u> at this level of performance.

What did baseball do that we don't do?

- Clearly defined the performance indicator (hit and get on base) related to the outcome (winning games)
- Observed performance and kept records
- Analyzed the data
- Developed a benchmark of excellence based on the analysis
- Publicized what they have learned (so the <u>public knows</u> that 30% is excellent)

Continuous Improvement?

There has been little change in the definition of excellence over all the time that baseball has been keeping statistics. There have been many attempts to improve performance during that time. However, whether manufacturing better bats, designing and building ball parks to favor hitters, changing the manufacture of the baseball to make it more "lively," or changing the height of the pitching mound, none of these has increased performance of the average baseball player to hit above .300 on a regular basis.

Is it reasonable to expect a 10% improvement every year in our field?

Participant Manual, "Introduction to ROMA" Version 5.0 © 2012 F. Richmond and B. Mooney, The Center for Applied Management Practices. Modified, from material © 1997- 2011, The Center for Applied Management Practices. Camp Hill, PA 717-730-3705, www.appliedmgt.com.

Activity – Success Measures in Industry

References for Setting Public and Nonprofit Sector Expectations

- Executive management recruitment, ____ % placement rate.

- New Magazines, ____ % survive over 12 months.

- Movies, One in ___ or ____ % make a profit.

- Broadway, One in ____ or ____ % make a profit.

- Music Recordings (CDs), ____% make a profit.

- Prescription drugs, ____ % make it to market.

- Of the prescription drugs that make it to the market, ____ % make a profit.

- Pfizer, One in ____ new drugs or ____% make it to the market, 10 – 12 years to develop a product.

- DuPont, One in ____ or ____% of ideas to generate one major marketable new product

- On Time Railroad Delivery + or - ____ hours.

- Baseball: 1 hit in 3 times at bat (.333 or 33%) is a superstar. 1 hit in 4 times at bat (.250 or 25%) is a successful hitter.

Community Action must establish its own standards of performance and communicate these standards of performance to elected officials, government, public and private funders, the general public, the media, and to the staff of CAAs and CSBG eligible entities.

Participant Manual, "Introduction to ROMA" Version 5.0 © 2012 F. Richmond and B. Mooney, The Center for Applied Management Practices. Modified, from material © 1997- 2011, The Center for Applied Management Practices. Camp Hill, PA 717-730-3705, www.appliedmgt.com.

Performance Targeting for NPIs — Another Way to Calculate Success

In addition to the performance related to the number of outcomes achieved compared to the number served, calculating agency performance for some of the items in the *National Performance Indicators* (NPIs) includes another dimension.

It is based on a different formula than the one we previously learned.

Performance in this case refers back to one of the key provisions of GPRA: <u>agencies must be able to accurately identify performance goals or targets prior to beginning service.</u> *(refer back to Module 1, p 4)*

"When reporting on the NPIs, CAAs are asked to project the number to be served and the number to achieve an outcome in three areas:
- National Performance Indicator 1.1 – Employment
- National Performance Indicator 1.3 – Economic Asset Enhancement and Utilization
- National Performance Indicator 6.3 – Child and Family Development

"The ability of local CAAs to <u>identify their own performance targets</u> continues to be of interest to the Administration, to the Congress and to the national network of CAAs.

"The activity of engaging in successful targeting fulfills an essential need for compliance with elements of the Government Performance and Results Act (GPRA) of 1993."

NASCSP FY 2009 NPI Instruction Manual

In this performance calculation, you will be comparing the number of <u>targeted or projected outcomes</u> (which becomes the denominator), with <u>the actual number who achieved those outcomes</u> (which becomes the numerator).

The calculation <u>does not use</u> the number of those <u>receiving services</u>.

This measurement is designed to identify the <u>ability of each CAA to project their performance</u>. Your ability to manage your program(s) effectively depends on your ability to accurately project how many outcomes you expect to document.

Another Dimension of Performance

In the example used previously, we projected that 7 out of the 20 families receiving case management services will achieve the expected outcome. This is the number projected – our target – and becomes the denominator of the fraction we are creating to establish this performance rate.

When the program was completed, we found that 5 families actually achieved the outcome. This actual number becomes the numerator of the fraction.

Your ability to successfully project your performance for this project is 71%.

(N) 5 families increase household income by 10% (Actual) = 71% success rate
(D) 7 families increase household income by 10% (Target)

State CSBG offices that collect the data to report to NASCSP are asked to provide follow-up explanations regarding any percent that is not within the range of 80% to 120%. In the example, our numbers are very small, but if we multiplied by 10 or 100, the difference between the target number and the actual number becomes more apparent. *If we projected 70 outcomes, the acceptable range of actual outcomes would be 56 to 84.*

What might be some reasons why an agency has under or over projected their outcomes?

OCS has forecasted that locally-determined performance targets will eventually apply to all of the NPIs. NASCSP has produced a manual to help states and local CAAs improve their performance targeting skills, titled *NASCSP Targeting Field Manual: Setting and Reviewing Targets*. This manual enables agencies to accurately predict and identify their results through detailed examples, tested strategies, case studies, and best practices. The Targeting Field Manual can be downloaded from the NASCSP web site.

Participant Manual, "Introduction to ROMA" Version 5.0 © 2012 F. Richmond and B. Mooney, The Center for Applied Management Practices. Modified, from material © 1997- 2011, The Center for Applied Management Practices. Camp Hill, PA 717-730-3705, www.appliedmgt.com.

Establishing Measurement Tools and Processes

When you are considering the outcomes you expect to achieve, you need to consider <u>how you will measure</u> the accomplishment of the outcomes. When we considered the identification of the indicator in the last module, we provided examples that included thinking about how you would measure the indicator. (For example: improved grades > report card) Now we need to look more closely at the measurement tools and processes that you will use as evidence.

Here are a few "short cuts" to help you.

---

1. Minimize Use of Soft Outcomes.

2. Use a Measurement Tool to Capture Outcomes.

3. Use a Pre-Existing Measurement Tool Before Creating One.

4. Research Other Organizations that May Have an Outcome Framework Before Creating Your Own.

Minimize Use of Soft Outcomes

Occasionally, agencies identify outcomes that are called "soft" outcomes because there is little "hard" data available to support these outcomes. Examples of "soft" outcomes include:

- <u>Achievement of self-esteem or self-confidence.</u> This is acceptable if it is part of an overall comprehensive assessment measuring other types of functioning as well.
- <u>Meeting or exceeding one's own goals</u>. This is sometimes identified as an outcome without identifying the goals. If you have a population who all have different goals, putting them together in this kind of "catch all" statement diminishes the value of the outcome.
- <u>Self-report of achieving an outcome</u>, without any objective backup.
- <u>Exclusive or inappropriate use of customer satisfaction surveys</u>. It is important if clients "like" the service, of course, but this cannot be the only measure of success.
- <u>Anecdotal stories</u> replacing hard or quantitative data. The use of personal stories can be very effective if they are part of a report that also has other data. But if they are the only measure of success, they may be limited in value.

Participant Manual, "Introduction to ROMA" Version 5.0 © 2012 F. Richmond and B. Mooney, The Center for Applied Management Practices. Modified, from material © 1997- 2011, The Center for Applied Management Practices. Camp Hill, PA 717-730-3705, www.appliedmgt.com.

Use a Measurement Tool to Capture Outcomes

A data collection or measurement tool must be identified that captures client data for each program or service:

- Intake and Assessment Instrument
- Pre- and Post-test.
- Customer/client satisfaction survey.
- Follow-up survey.
- Observational survey.
- Scale, e.g., functioning scale or self-sufficiency scale.

Use a Preexisting Measurement Tool before Creating One

There are existing tools that may be available for measuring outcomes. CAAs should be encouraged to use these existing outcome measurement tools before creating their own. These are just a few examples available to the network.

Education programs, such as Adult Basic Education (ABE) and English as a Second Language (ESL), have standardized outcome measurement tools available. Counseling and behavior modification programs also have tools to measure changes in function such as the Global Assessment of Functioning Scale (GAF). Standardized tools are also available for employment and training.

Research Other Organizations That May Have an Outcome Framework Before Creating Your Own.

There are many organizations with national affiliations that have made significant investments in their outcome evaluation and reporting systems. Rather than duplicate work, efforts should be made to use the same outcomes and measures that these organizations report to their regional affiliates or national headquarters. Organizations believed to have national outcome evaluation and reporting requirements include:

- American Red Cross
- Big Brothers Big Sisters
- Boys and Girls Clubs
- Girl Scouts, Boy Scouts
- Salvation Army
- United Way
- YMCA, YWCA

Faith-based organizations such as Catholic Social Services, Lutheran Services, and Jewish Family Services may also use standardized measurement tools. Other government agencies, such as HUD, also have standardized measures.

Participant Manual, "Introduction to ROMA" Version 5.0 © 2012 F. Richmond and B. Mooney, The Center for Applied Management Practices. Modified, from material © 1997- 2011, The Center for Applied Management Practices. Camp Hill, PA 717-730-3705, www.appliedmgt.com.

Identifying Evidence

Drucker reminded us that, just like we looked at qualitative and quantitative need data, we will identify both qualitative and quantitative measures.

From "What are our results? Question Four" (p. 41)

"Progress and achievement can be appraised in *qualitative* and *quantitative* terms. These two types of measures are interwoven – they shed light on one another – and both are necessary to illuminate in what ways and to what extent lives are being changed."

- "Qualitative measures address <u>the depth and breadth of change</u> within a particular context. Qualitative results can be in the realm of the intangible, such as instilling hope in a patient battling cancer…. Qualitative data, although sometimes more subjective and difficult to grasp, are just as real, just as important, and can be gathered just as systematically as the quantitative."

- "Quantitative measures <u>use defined standards</u>. Quantitative appraisal offers valid hard data. Quantitative measures are essential for assessing whether resources are properly concentrated for results, whether progress is being made, whether lives and communities are changing for the better."

We must have a clear idea about what we will measure (our outcome indicator) and also about how we will measure the results — about the evidence we will use to support our claims of success.

Think about the question: "How do you know?"
> What proof can you provide that an outcome has been achieved?
> What documentation do you have?

Participant Manual, "Introduction to ROMA" Version 5.0 © 2012 F. Richmond and B. Mooney, The Center for Applied Management Practices. Modified, from material © 1997- 2011, The Center for Applied Management Practices. Camp Hill, PA 717-730-3705, www.appliedmgt.com.

Activity – What Are Our Measurement Tools and Processes?

Instructions: Consider the needs, outcomes, strategies, and outcome indicators you identified previously.

What measurement tools will you use to document your results?	Who will be responsible? How will the data be collected?	What is the frequency of data collection and reporting?

Logic Model

1	2	3	4	5	6	7	8
N	S	O	OI		M	D	F
Mission:							

Participant Manual, "Introduction to ROMA" Version 5.0 © 2012 F. Richmond and B. Mooney, The Center for Applied Management Practices. Modified, from material © 1997- 2011, The Center for Applied Management Practices. Camp Hill, PA 717-730-3705, www.appliedmgt.com.

Module Six

Observing Achievement of Results Using Scales and Matrices

Introduction to Outcome Scales
Scale Methodology Developed by the MATF
Activity – Developing a Housing Scale – Part One
Activity – Developing a Housing Scale – Part Two
Analysis of Sample Housing Scale
Sample Housing Scale
Establishing Placement on a Scale
Sample Assessment Questions for Placement on a Scale
Uses of an Outcome Scale
Measuring Progress and Reporting Using Outcome Scales
Activity – Create an Outcome Scale
Outcome Scale Template
Introduction to the Outcome Matrix
Characteristics of an Outcome Matrix
Sample Outcome Matrix
Sample Family Outcome Matrix
Activity – Analysis of a Family Outcome Matrix

Learning Objectives:

- Participants learn the process of creating an outcome scale.
- Participants understand how outcome scales can be used to measure incremental change and movement towards self-sufficiency.
- Participants are able to combine outcome scales to form *An Outcome Matrix* to capture multiple interventions, needs, programs, and outcomes.
- Participants understand the uses of the Outcome Matrix and can analyze an Outcome Matrix.

Participant Manual, "Introduction to ROMA" Version 5.0 © 2012 F. Richmond and B. Mooney, The Center for Applied Management Practices. Modified, from material © 1997- 2011, The Center for Applied Management Practices. Camp Hill, PA 717-730-3705, www.appliedmgt.com.

Introduction to Outcome Scales

**An Outcome Scale is
a continuum that describes different states or conditions of status.**

An automobile gas gauge is one example of a very simple scale.

```
F
¾
½
¼
E
```

Without having the definitions of the above labels (F, ¾, ½, ¼, E), we can recognize a continuum ranging from most desirable status, F, to least desirable status, E.

Outcome scales are used to identify and measure incremental change.

We keep our eye on the gas gauge because it shows the changing amount of gas in the tank as indicated by placement on the "scale."

The Outcome Scale used in Community Action is a five-point continuum of outcomes that describes different states or conditions of status ranging from Thriving to In-Crisis.

It can be used to identify and assess or measure incremental change in families, agencies, and communities.

Participant Manual, "Introduction to ROMA" Version 5.0 © 2012 F. Richmond and B. Mooney, The Center for Applied Management Practices. Modified, from material © 1997- 2011, The Center for Applied Management Practices. Camp Hill, PA 717-730-3705, www.appliedmgt.com.

Scale Methodology Developed by the Monitoring and Assessment Task Force

A five-point scale template was developed by the CSBG Monitoring and Assessment Task Force (MATF) in the early 1990s.

The MATF provided some examples of scales, but did not define the benchmarks to be adopted by all CAAs. The MATF believed it best to have the outcomes associated with each benchmark be <u>developed by local consensus,</u> which served to define the terms.

- Thriving

- Safe

- Stable

Prevention Line _____

- Vulnerable

- In-Crisis

Early work in creating samples of definitions associated with scale benchmarks in multiple domains was done by Frederick Richmond. For example, The Family Self Sufficiency Scale was developed in Pennsylvania in 1995 by the Bucks County Opportunity Council and Richmond. The MATF "Scales and Ladders" Committee and others throughout the country (such as the IL Community Action Association) also worked on providing local agencies with sample scales beginning at that time.

See www.roma1.org for these and other examples.

Participant Manual, "Introduction to ROMA" Version 5.0 © 2012 F. Richmond and B. Mooney, The Center for Applied Management Practices. Modified, from material © 1997- 2011, The Center for Applied Management Practices. Camp Hill, PA 717-730-3705, www.appliedmgt.com.

Activity — Developing a Housing Outcome Scale — Part One

Instructions: Think about all the various types of housing conditions. Jot down the possibilities here.
Consider a range of all housing, both best and worst-case scenarios

Participant Manual, "Introduction to ROMA" Version 5.0 © 2012 F. Richmond and B. Mooney, The Center for Applied Management Practices. Modified, from material © 1997- 2011, The Center for Applied Management Practices. Camp Hill, PA 717-730-3705, www.appliedmgt.com.

Activity — Developing a Housing Outcome Scale — Part Two

Instructions: In the template below, transfer your housing conditions from the previous page alongside the benchmarks that best describes the condition.

Benchmarks	Outcomes
Thriving	
Safe	
Stable	
Prevention Line	
Vulnerable	
In-Crisis	

Stop!!   Stop!!   Stop!!

Please do not turn to the next page which contains a sample completed Housing Outcome Scale. Review this only after you have completed this exercise.

Participant Manual, "Introduction to ROMA" Version 5.0 © 2012 F. Richmond and B. Mooney, The Center for Applied Management Practices. Modified, from material © 1997- 2011, The Center for Applied Management Practices. Camp Hill, PA 717-730-3705, www.appliedmgt.com.

Analysis of the Sample Housing Scale

<u>Please note:</u> This is <u>one</u> example of a Housing Scale. It is not to be considered the "correct" scale, as the descriptors contained in the benchmarks should be based on local conditions.

Factors to consider:

- The type of Outcome Scale you create for your community may be different from other communities. In all likelihood, it will take negotiators within the group who will identify the conditions (outcomes) and where to associate them to the scale benchmarks. For example, public housing could be associated in any of the five scale benchmarks depending on the location, quality of housing, conditions in the neighborhood, etc. Outcome statements are written to <u>approximate actual conditions</u>, and the placement of the conditions on the benchmarks <u>must be accepted by all</u> who use the scale.

- Some Outcome Scales include headers associated with each benchmark to help decide where to place the outcomes. Such as "limited choice" or "dangerous."

- Within a benchmark, when there is more than one outcome, you have two situations: either the outcomes can have the same value such as in Stable (6A, 6B, 6C) or different values such as In-Crisis (2, 1A, 1B, 0). Only one outcome is placed in each outcome benchmark <u>unless</u> assigned an individual score. Numbers provide a shortcut to understanding placement on an Outcome Scale within benchmarks.

- There is a significant difference in outcomes placed in the "Vulnerable" and "Stable" benchmarks. Movement from "Vulnerable" to "Stable" is the <u>transition from dependence to independence.</u>

- In this model, a score of 5 or greater indicates placement above the Prevention Line. Outcomes <u>above</u> the prevention line are considered achievements of <u>independence.</u> Outcomes <u>below</u> the prevention line are considered conditions of <u>dependence.</u>

Participant Manual, "Introduction to ROMA" Version 5.0 © 2012 F. Richmond and B. Mooney, The Center for Applied Management Practices. Modified, from material © 1997- 2011, The Center for Applied Management Practices. Camp Hill, PA 717-730-3705, www.appliedmgt.com.

Sample Housing Scale

Outcome Level   ☑ Family ☐ Agency ☐ Community

Benchmarks	Outcomes
Thriving (9-10) **Independent**	Housing of Choice – Non-Subsidized Safe and secure non-subsidized housing of choice (Home, Condominium, Co-Op); <u>owner.</u> (10A) Safe and secure non-subsidized housing of choice; <u>renter.</u> (10B)
Safe (7-8) **Independent**	Limited Choice of Housing – Non-Subsidized Safe and secure non-subsidized housing; <u>choices</u> <u>limited</u> due to moderate income; <u>owner.</u> (8A) Safe and secure non-subsidized housing; <u>choices</u> <u>limited</u> due to moderate income; <u>renter.</u> (8B)
Stable (5-6) (May include elements of dependency) **Independent**	Limited Choice of Housing – Subsidized Safe and secure Section 8 housing. (6A) Safe and secure <u>subsidized</u> rental apartment. (6B) Safe and secure public housing. (6C) Safe and secure <u>permanent</u> living arrangements with others. (5)
	Prevention Line
Vulnerable (3-4) **Dependent**	Temporary Housing or At-Risk of Losing Housing Safe and secure <u>transitional</u> housing (for 60 days). (4A) Living with others – <u>temporary</u> arrangements. (4B) <u>Unaffordable</u> ownership or rental. (3)
In-Crisis (0-2) **Dependent**	Dangerous or No Housing Safe shelter (for 30 days). (2A) Notice of mortgage foreclosure. (2B) <u>Unsafe</u> Shelter. (1A) <u>Substandard</u> or <u>unsafe</u> ownership or rental. (1B) Homeless. (0)

<u>Hint:</u> **It is often helpful to view the top end of the scale as the "best" case scenario, and the lowest end of the scale as the "worst" case scenario.**

Participant Manual, "Introduction to ROMA" Version 5.0 © 2012 F. Richmond and B. Mooney, The Center for Applied Management Practices. Modified, from material © 1997- 2011, The Center for Applied Management Practices. Camp Hill, PA 717-730-3705, www.appliedmgt.com.

Establishing Placement on a Scale

It is important to establish a standardized procedure for placing a client on an Outcome Scale. Once the benchmark definitions are agreed upon, everyone who uses the scale must use the same definitions for each benchmark.

Any interview, client assessment, and subsequent placement on an Outcome Scale, must be done in an <u>objective manner</u>. The best way to standardize placement on an Outcome Scale is to have an associated assessment tool with statements specific to the scale outcomes.

On the next page, you will see <u>an example of questions</u> that could be used to relate to an Outcome Scale. Since a client can only be in one place at one time on an Outcome Scale, the client would be asked to choose the statement that <u>best represents</u> the present situation or condition.

You will see the questions that would be asked of the client in <u>Column 1</u>, the related benchmark in <u>Column (2)</u>, and where the client would be placed on the Housing Scale in <u>Column (3)</u>. Only the information in Column 1 would be provided to the client for response. In this manner, the assessment is administered without the benchmarks and scale elements shown, as they may influence a "judgment" rather than an objective placement.

It is also important to consider how you might document the placement (what evidence you would use to support the placement). Some agencies use "client report" for initial placement. In these cases, it is good practice to have the ability to go back and adjust the intake information if additional data are acquired that would challenge the original placement.

It is difficult to accurately measure movement on a scale if the initial placement is faulty. You must have a reliable way to establish the baseline.

An assessment comprised of associated statements would be developed for each Outcome Scale used in the agency.

Participant Manual, "Introduction to ROMA" Version 5.0 © 2012 F. Richmond and B. Mooney, The Center for Applied Management Practices. Modified, from material © 1997- 2011, The Center for Applied Management Practices. Camp Hill, PA 717-730-3705, www.appliedmgt.com.

Sample Assessment Questions for Placement on a Housing Scale

Choose the one statement that best describes your current housing (1)	Benchmarks (2)	Housing Scale (3)
☐ I own and live in a house without a mortgage. ☐ I live in a condominium or co-op without a mortgage. ☐ I rent an unsubsidized apartment of my choice ☐ I live in a home and pay the mortgage without assistance. --	Thriving	Home Ownership (10A) Condominium Ownership (10B) Co-Op Home Ownership 10C) Non-subsidized rental housing (10D)
☐ I live in a home and pay the mortgage without assistance, but my income limits my choice of where I live. ☐ I live in an apartment and pay rent without assistance, but my income limits my choice of where I live. --	Safe	Safe and secure non-subsidized housing, choices limited due to moderate income, homeowner. (8A) Safe and secure non-subsidized housing, choices limited due to moderate income, renter. (8B)
☐ I live in safe and secure subsidized Section 8 housing. I can afford the rent payments. ☐ I live in a safe and secure subsidized rental apartment that I can afford. ☐ I live in safe and secure subsidized public housing that I can afford. ☐ I live with others as a choice (shared housing, shared responsibilities) --	Stable	Safe and secure subsidized Section 8 housing. (6A) Safe and secure subsidized rental apartment. (6B) Safe and secure subsidized public housing. (6C) Shared Housing of choice(5)
	Prevention Line	
☐ I live in safe and secure transitional housing. ☐ I live in a home I cannot afford. ☐ I live in a non-subsidized rental apartment I cannot afford. ☐ I live in a subsidized rental apartment I cannot afford. ☐ I live in a temporary shelter. --	Vulnerable	Safe and secure transitional housing. (4) Unaffordable home (3A) Unaffordable non-subsidized rental (3B) Unaffordable subsidized rental (3C) Temporary shelter (3D)
☐ I am living with relatives or friends because I have no choice. ☐ I live in a substandard or unsafe house or apartment. ☐ I am homeless.	In-Crisis	Living with others (no choice) (2A) Notice of mortgage foreclosure (2B) Substandard or unsafe housing (1) Homeless (0)

Note: Alternate shading in Column 3 was used to visually distinguish the outcome statements from each other.

Participant Manual, "Introduction to ROMA" Version 5.0 © 2012 F. Richmond and B. Mooney, The Center for Applied Management Practices. Modified, from material © 1997- 2011, The Center for Applied Management Practices. Camp Hill, PA 717-730-3705, www.appliedmgt.com.

Using Outcome Scales

Outcome Scales have been recognized for many decades by disciplines in the health and social services fields when it is important to measure functioning and incremental change.

For example, Outcome Scales have been used in Mental Health to determine if it is appropriate to move a client from a more restrictive to less restrictive setting, or to discharge from a hospital, back into the community. The data collected and analyzed from placement on an outcome scale such as this support the management of the patient/client and improved decision-making.

In Community Action, Outcome Scales are used to measure incremental change between the scale benchmarks which allow us to "document" the movement from conditions of dependency to increasing self-sufficiency.

Outcome Scales can be used to:
- help visualize the "big picture" of the situation facing the client at first meeting,
- measure change by comparing scale placement at two or more different times indicating positive or negative change or no change characterized as neutral or stable,
- determine how much progress and the time it takes an individual to reach the next scale benchmark,
- capture incremental change, interim success, and progress towards long-term goals as interim goals are achieved,
- identify areas where progress has not been made towards achieving long-term goals,
- recognize any movement in a positive direction on the outcome scale as movement toward self-sufficiency even if the movement is from "In-Crisis" to "Vulnerable," and
- support development of a case management plan where the client and worker establish mutually agreeable goals for movement towards self-sufficiency.

The graphic nature of the Outcome Scale makes it an effective tool to help visualize progress towards self-sufficiency.

Participant Manual, "Introduction to ROMA" Version 5.0 © 2012 F. Richmond and B. Mooney, The Center for Applied Management Practices. Modified, from material © 1997- 2011, The Center for Applied Management Practices. Camp Hill, PA 717-730-3705, www.appliedmgt.com.

Measuring Progress and Reporting Using an Outcome Scale

As client progress is observed or reported, it is good practice to document this movement by noting the new status on the scale. Each benchmark on the outcome scale has associated outcomes. It is the change in status, movement from one outcome to another, which needs to be documented and reported. It is also important to document and report where there is no change.

Consider the kind of evidence or documentation that would be used to verify client progress.

It is the individual benchmarks or outcomes on the Outcome Scale that are the reportable outcomes, not the labels "Thriving" to "In-Crisis."

It is not appropriate to report outside the program that the client "moved up" one benchmark on the outcome scale since movement from one benchmark to another will mean different things for each agency.

In the Housing example, you would not report that the person moved up two benchmarks from In-Crisis to Safe. You would report that the person acquired permanent "Safe and secure non-subsidized housing," a measurable outcome.

Note: Many software and electronic data collection systems include scales, or these can be embedded.

Participant Manual, "Introduction to ROMA" Version 5.0 © 2012 F. Richmond and B. Mooney, The Center for Applied Management Practices. Modified, from material © 1997- 2011, The Center for Applied Management Practices. Camp Hill, PA 717-730-3705, www.appliedmgt.com.

Activity – Create an Outcome Scale

> **Instructions:** Create a work or personal outcome scale. Start by framing the conditions from best to worst or worst to best case. When you use these please *leave the footer intact.*

Outcome Scale Template

Program/Service/Activity:_____

Outcome Level: ☐ Family ☐ Agency ☐ Community

Benchmarks	Outcomes
Thriving **Independent**	
Safe **Independent**	
Stable **Independent**	
	Prevention Line
Vulnerable **Dependent**	
In-Crisis **Dependent**	

Hint: It is often helpful to view the top end of the scale as the "best" case scenario, and the lowest end of the scale as the "worst" case scenario.

Participant Manual, "Introduction to ROMA" Version 5.0 © 2012 F. Richmond and B. Mooney, The Center for Applied Management Practices. Modified, from material © 1997- 2011, The Center for Applied Management Practices. Camp Hill, PA 717-730-3705, www.appliedmgt.com.

Introduction to the Outcome Matrix

As we have seen, the Outcome Scale helps measure incremental change in a single category or domain. Think of the previous example of a Housing Scale. We can measure change by first administering an assessment at the initiation of service resulting in a <u>baseline</u> placement on a scale to identify the starting point. Any subsequent assessment and placement on the Outcome Scale is then compared to the baseline which yields three possibilities: <u>a positive change, negative change, or no change.</u>

In the human condition, we know "well-being" or achieving a level of self-sufficiency depends on the <u>congruence of multiple factors</u> that allow us to be functional on a daily basis.

In general, we accept the need for families to have a wage earner bringing in sufficient income to meet the expenses of the household. We accept that adult family members must have sufficient education and/or skills to provide for good housing, food, transportation, childcare (if needed), discretionary spending, etc. If we are thinking about an Outcome Scale, we would visualize these factors <u>above</u> the Prevention Line.

At its simplest, an Outcome Matrix is a grouping of Outcome Scales arranged side by side.

When we select a number of scales that most relate to the overall circumstance that we are interested in measuring, we create an Outcome Matrix. The choice of the various Outcome Scales that comprise an Outcome Matrix will affect the data you collect and analyze and the story you wish to tell. For example, an "employment" program may want to include scales related to Education, Childcare, and Transportation. A "parent education" program may want to include scales related to Parent/Child Interaction, Food and Nutrition, and Health. A "case management" program may select scales related to Income, Housing, Financial Literacy, and Asset Development.

Note: Bill Hamilton, Community Action Marin, San Rafael, CA, was an early developer of the outcome matrix concept. He produced matrices in all three levels (family, agency, and community) in January 1995, which were used as an aid to planning. The focus of the matrix and the labels on the rows and columns were changed by Richmond for use in implementing ROMA. He created the Bucks County Family Self Sufficiency Matrix in 1995.

Participant Manual, "Introduction to ROMA" Version 5.0 © 2012 F. Richmond and B. Mooney, The Center for Applied Management Practices. Modified, from material © 1997- 2011, The Center for Applied Management Practices. Camp Hill, PA 717-730-3705, www.appliedmgt.com.

Characteristics of an Outcome Matrix

By using a common framework, outcome scales combined into an outcome matrix can be aggregated and provide a multidimensional look at the agency's work. Aggregation is important because it allows <u>agencies</u> to present data on a number of clients and programs in a uniform and quantifiable manner.

An outcome matrix is used to:

- capture a client's progress (incremental change) <u>across more than one scale</u> (program or service) and <u>over time</u>,

- capture the data by client <u>across all agency programs</u> and services in addition to capturing data by <u>each program or service</u>. This allows for an unduplicated count.

- analyze data by <u>both</u> client and program,

- identify where the client <u>has strengths</u> (above the prevention line) and where the client <u>needs improvement</u> (below the prevention line),

- identify <u>the relationship between different</u> domains of a problem or where outcome scales interrelate,

- provide the <u>background context</u> for explaining the agency's actions and strategies,

- create a framework for reporting,

- adjust <u>agency resource allocation</u> to areas where it will be the most efficient and effective (where the problem is), and

- create a <u>mini-needs assessment</u> based on the "experience" of the client population.

Participant Manual, "Introduction to ROMA" Version 5.0 © 2012 F. Richmond and B. Mooney, The Center for Applied Management Practices. Modified, from material © 1997- 2011, The Center for Applied Management Practices. Camp Hill, PA 717-730-3705, www.appliedmgt.com.

Sample Outcome Matrix

In the Outcome Matrix presented on the next page, you will find six areas which an agency may use to <u>define "well being" of a family</u>.

- Income
- Employment
- Housing
- Education and Training
- Transportation
- Childcare

This sample shows the placement of a family on the matrix at three time periods (Feb. 1, May 1, Aug. 1). The status at the time of placement is highlighted.

Other models of matrices have selected different domains, with some matrices having 20 or more scales. In the model developed by The Center for Applied Management Practices, Inc., there are nine domains in which outcome scales are organized. These nine domains are comparable to the CSBG categories.

Outcome Matrix	CSBG Categories
Education and Training	Education Programs
Employment	Employment Programs
Financial Literacy	Income Management Programs
Food and Nutrition	Nutrition Programs
Health	Health Programs
Housing	Housing Programs
Human Services	Emergency Services, and Youth and Seniors Programs
Income	Self-Sufficiency Programs
Transportation	

Note: This is a Family Matrix and the CSBG Categories of "Linkages" is more appropriately found in an Agency and Community Matrices, so it is not included in the list.

See www.roma-nptp.org for samples of community and agency matrices.

Participant Manual, "Introduction to ROMA" Version 5.0 © 2012 F. Richmond and B. Mooney, The Center for Applied Management Practices. Modified, from material © 1997- 2011, The Center for Applied Management Practices. Camp Hill, PA 717-730-3705, www.appliedmgt.com.

Sample Family Outcome Matrix – 1st Assessment–Feb. 1, 2nd Assessment–May 1, 3rd Assessment–Aug. 1

The status of the client is the placement on the scale directly above the date which is gray shaded, bolded, and dated. The 1st assessment is Feb 1. Subsequent assessments on May 1 and Aug 1 follow the same format.

Domains / Benchmarks	Income	Employment	Housing	Education and Training	Transportation	Childcare
Thriving (9-10)	> 200% of poverty adjusted for family size. (10)	Full-time work above minimum wage with employer-provided benefits. (10)	Home Ownership (10A) Condominium Ownership (10B) Co-Op Home Ownership 10C) Non-subsidized rental housing (10D)	Post-Secondary degree: Masters or doctorate. (10) / Post-Secondary degree: bachelors, associates. (9)	Family members always have transportation needs met through public transportation, a car, or a regular ride. (10)	Child enrolled in unsubsidized, licensed childcare setting of own choice. (10)-Aug 1
Safe (8-9)	Between 176%-200% of poverty adjusted for family size. (8) — May 1	**Full-time work above minimum wage without employer-provided benefits. (8)-Aug 1**	Safe and secure non-subsidized housing, choices limited due to moderate income, homeowner. (8A) / Safe and secure non-subsidized housing, choices limited due to moderate income, renter. (8B)	Post high school vocational education, non college business, or technical or vocational training, or some college credits	**Family members have most transportation needs met through public transportation, a car, or a regular ride. (8)-Aug 1** — Aug 1	Child enrolled in licensed, subsidized childcare of own choice. (8) / **Child enrolled in licensed, subsidized childcare, limited choice. (7)-May 1 & Aug 1** — May 1 / Aug 1
Stable (5-6)	**Between 126%-175% of poverty adjusted for family size. (6)-Aug 1** — Aug 1	Full-time work at minimum wage with employer-provided benefits. (6)-8/1 / **Full-time work at minimum wage without employer-provided benefits. (5)-May 1** — Aug 1 / May 1	Safe and secure subsidized Section 8 housing. (6A) / **Safe and secure subsidized rental apartment. (6B)-Aug 1** / Safe and secure subsidized public housing. (6C) — Aug 1	**High school diploma or G.E.D. (6)-Feb 1, May 1 & Aug 1** — Feb. 1 / May 1 / Aug 1	**Family members have some transportation needs met through public transportation, a car, or a regular ride. (6)-May 1** — May 1	Child provided childcare by a family member or friend. (6) / Child provided childcare by various caregivers (5)
	Prevention Line	Prevention Line	Prevention Line		Prevention Line	
Vulnerable (3-4)	**Between 100%-125% of poverty adjusted for family size. (4)-May 1** — May 1	Part-time employment with benefits. (4)-5/1 / **Part-time employment without benefits. (3)-Feb 1** — Feb 1	**Safe and secure transitional housing. (4)-Feb 1 & May 1** / Unaffordable home (3A) / Unaffordable rental (3B) / Temporary shelter (3C) — Feb. 1 / May 1	Reading, writing, and basic math skills present, no high school diploma or G.E.D. (4)	**Family members rarely have transportation needs met through public transportation, a car, or a regular ride. (3)-Feb 1** — Feb. 1	**Child on waiting list for enrollment in childcare. (3)-Feb 1**
In-Crisis (0-2)	**Between 50%-100% of poverty (by family size.) (2)-Feb 1** / Between 0% - 49% of poverty by family size (0) — Feb. 1	Unemployed with work history and skills. (2)-2/1 / Unemployed without work history or skills(0) — Feb 1	Living with relatives (2) / Substandard or unsafe housing (1) / Homeless (0) — Feb. 1 / May 1	Reading, writing, and basic math skills absent. (0)	Family members do not have public transportation, a car, or regular ride. (0) — Feb. 1	Child not enrolled in childcare. (2) / Child enrolled in unregulated or unlicensed childcare facility. (0) — Feb. 1

Participant Manual, "Introduction to ROMA" Version 5.0 © 2012 F. Richmond and B. Mooney, The Center for Applied Management Practices. Modified, from material © 1997- 2011, The Center for Applied Management Practices. Camp Hill, PA 717-730-3705, www.appliedmgt.com.

93

Participant Manual, "Introduction to ROMA" Version 5.0 © 2012 F. Richmond and B. Mooney, The Center for Applied Management Practices. Modified, from material © 1997- 2011, The Center for Applied Management Practices. Camp Hill, PA 717-730-3705, www.appliedmgt.com.

Activity – Analysis of a
Family Outcome Matrix

In the preceding outcome matrix, the client was assessed in six areas: Income, Employment, Housing, Education and Training, Transportation, and Childcare.

Instructions: Please take five minutes and analyze the family outcome matrix by yourself. Identify at least four changes that have occurred in the status of the client/family. After you have analyzed the matrix, participate in a small group discussion and prepare an overall assessment of the changes that have taken place since the initial intake on February 1st. Identify a spokesperson to present your group work to the class. Please take notes below:

Income:

Employment:

Housing:

Education:

Transportation:

Childcare:

Overall Assessment:

Participant Manual, "Introduction to ROMA" Version 5.0 © 2012 F. Richmond and B. Mooney, The Center for Applied Management Practices. Modified, from material © 1997- 2011, The Center for Applied Management Practices. Camp Hill, PA 717-730-3705, www.appliedmgt.com.

Module Seven

Managing Performance with the Logic Model

Learning Objectives:
- Participants will learn how to construct and use a ROMA Logic Model.
- Participants will identify short, intermediate, and long-term outcomes on logic models and how these relate to scales.
- Participants will understand how analysis of data in a logic model can lead to improved program management and decision-making.
- Participants will understand how logic models can assist in the targeting process.
- Participants compare the features of the eLogic Model® to the traditional logic model.

Participant Manual, "Introduction to ROMA" Version 5.0 © 2012 F. Richmond and B. Mooney, The Center for Applied Management Practices. Modified, from material © 1997- 2011, The Center for Applied Management Practices. Camp Hill, PA 717-730-3705, www.appliedmgt.com.

Understanding the Logic Model

Bringing It All Together with the Logic Model

We have been "building" the logic model throughout the Modules, looking at the principles and practices behind each of the columns, and now we will look at the entire Logic Model.

The logic model is a ROMA tool that links <u>program</u> <u>operations,</u> and <u>program</u> <u>accountability.</u>

- <u>Program</u> <u>operations,</u> in Columns 1-5 of the logic model, include mission, need, intervention, projected results, and actual results.

- <u>Program</u> <u>accountability,</u> in Columns 6-8 of the logic model include the measurement tool(s), data source, and frequency of data collection and reporting including personnel assigned to each function.

The logic model can be used to support planning, monitoring, evaluation, and other management and accountability functions of the agency.

Activity: Does the information "match?"

The information in the columns of the Logic Model must "match" — must be connected in realistic and appropriate ways. You will be given some sample information to review.

Decide if the outcome identified meets the stated need, if the service will produce the outcome, the indicator can be measured, the measurement tool will produce evidence, and if appropriate personnel and procedures are identified.

Participant Manual, "Introduction to ROMA" Version 5.0 © 2012 F. Richmond and B. Mooney, The Center for Applied Management Practices. Modified, from material © 1997- 2011, The Center for Applied Management Practices. Camp Hill, PA 717-730-3705, www.appliedmgt.com.

Building a Logic Model

A. Identify the <u>name of the program</u> or service at the top of the logic model.
B. Identify whether it is a <u>family, agency, or community</u> logic model.
C. Write the <u>mission statement</u> for the program or service.
D. Fill out the Columns:

- **Identify the Need, problem, or situation** to be addressed in Col. 1.

- **Identify the Service or activity** that is expected to produce the outcome. In Column 2, identify the service or activity, the number of clients estimated to be served, or number of units to be offered, and a timeframe.

- **Identify the Outcome.** In Column 3, write the broad statement(s) about the outcome that is expected, <u>without</u> numbers or a percentage.

- **Identify the Outcome/Indicator.** In Column 4, write the outcome/indicator(s) that matches the outcome(s) in Column 3 that you **estimate, or project.** This includes the total number of clients who are <u>expected to achieve the outcome</u> within the established timeframe, stated as a fraction (using this number as the <u>numerator</u> and the number expected to receive the service as the <u>denominator</u>).

- **After the service has been delivered** you will identify the <u>actual number who achieved the outcome</u> within the established timeframe, and the actual number of clients who received the service. In Column 5, enter the number of clients who achieved the outcome/indicator, and calculate the actual percent of success. As in Column 4, this is <u>stated as a fraction</u> (with the number achieving the outcome as the numerator and the number who received the service as the denominator).

- **Identify the Measurement Tool.** In Column 6, identify the type of tool used to collect or measure the outcome.

- **Identify the Data Sources, Collection Procedures, and Personnel.** In Column 7, describe the sources of data, how it is collected, and staff assigned to the task(s). Be explicit and provide detail both for activity inside and external to the agency.

- **Determine the Frequency of Data Collection and Reporting.** In Column 8, describe how often data is collected and reported within and outside the agency. Provide explicit detail and documentation for this process.

E. Indicate if a <u>Proxy Outcome</u> is used in the Logic Model.

Participant Manual, "Introduction to ROMA" Version 5.0 © 2012 F. Richmond and B. Mooney, The Center for Applied Management Practices. Modified, from material © 1997- 2011, The Center for Applied Management Practices. Camp Hill, PA 717-730-3705, www.appliedmgt.com.

Activity – Building a Logic Model
Part One

Building Your Own Logic Model.

There are two blank logic models on the following pages. One is for this activity and the other can be kept for future use. If you use this logic model template in your work, please keep the footer intact.

Instructions: Begin building your logic model by considering a program that you know. Identify the program name and the program mission statement. Enter these on the logic model template.

Starting on the left side of the logic model template, identify <u>the need</u> in Column One. In Column Two, identify the specific service.

Writing Outcomes and Indicators.

You have the opportunity to practice creating outcome language and identifying the outcome indicator(s) that identifies that the outcome(s) has been achieved. In Column Three, identify the outcome. In Column Four, identify the outcome indicators for the service.

Notes:
- If this was an actual activity and not an exercise, you would have already identified need, services, outcomes, and outcome indicators from your strategic planning efforts. During these efforts, you would have first identified the outcomes followed by the services, if you were using the ROMA model outlined in previous modules. Think of this activity as if you are "transferring" your previous work to a graphic presentation.

- Avoid using proxy outcomes in this assignment. You will mark "none" in the proxy box.

- Please use family level outcomes for this activity. Mark the form in the appropriate place.

Identify a spokesperson to present your group work to the class.

Participant Manual, "Introduction to ROMA" Version 5.0 © 2012 F. Richmond and B. Mooney, The Center for Applied Management Practices. Modified, from material © 1997- 2011, The Center for Applied Management Practices. Camp Hill, PA 717-730-3705, www.appliedmgt.com.

Activity – Building a Logic Model
Part Two

Measuring and Documenting Results

Instructions: Using the work just completed for Columns 1-4, decide how you will measure, document, and report on your program. You will be completing Columns 6, 7, and 8.

Identify the <u>Measurement Tool</u>, form, or other medium where raw data are collected, and enter it in Column 6.

Identify the <u>Data Source, Data Collection Procedures, and Personnel Needed for Data Collection,</u> and enter it in Column 7. This refers to the place where data are maintained, i.e., individual case records, central database, a specialized database. It can also refer to the actual location, i.e., on-site, with a subcontractor, or online. The collection procedures will need to describe the method(s) for retrieving data from the data source(s), i.e., data from case records are retrieved manually while data are maintained in an automated database that may be accessed electronically. The final question is about the personnel who will be (or who are) assigned to the task.

Identify the Frequency of both Data Collection and Reporting and enter it in Column 8. This refers to how often data are required to be collected, and how often data are reported.

Identify a group spokesperson to present your work on Columns 6, 7, and 8 to the class.

<u>Please Note:</u> Why have we skipped Column Five?
That is the Actual Results Column, which is completed <u>after</u> the service is provided and the data are collected.

99

Participant Manual, "Introduction to ROMA" Version 5.0 © 2012 F. Richmond and B. Mooney, The Center for Applied Management Practices. Modified, from material © 1997- 2011, The Center for Applied Management Practices. Camp Hill, PA 717-730-3705, www.appliedmgt.com.

ROMA Logic Model
National ROMA Peer-To-Peer Training Program

Organization: _____ Program: _____ ☐ Family ☐ Agency ☐ Community

Identified Need, Problem, Situation	Service or Activity	Outcome	Indicator	Actual Results	Measurement Tool	Data Source	Frequency of Data Collection and Reporting
	Identify the # of clients to be served. Identify the time frame for the project. *May also include the # of units of service offered.*	General statement of results expected	Projected # of clients expected to achieve each outcome divided by the number served; the % expected to achieve	The **Actual** # of clients achieving the outcome, divided by the number served; the % of clients who achieved each outcome.	What evidence will you collect to prove your outcomes were achieved?	Include Collection Procedure, Personnel Responsible	
(1) Planning	(2) Intervention	(3) Benefit	(4) Performance	(5) Performance	(6) Accountability	(7) Accountability	(8) Accountability

Mission: _____

Proxy Outcome: _____

Participant Manual, "Introduction to ROMA" Version 5.0 © 2012 F. Richmond and B. Mooney, The Center for Applied Management Practices. Modified, from material © 1997- 2011, The Center for Applied Management Practices. Camp Hill, PA 717-730-3705, www.appliedmgt.com.

ROMA Logic Model
National ROMA Peer-To-Peer Training Program

□ Family □ Agency □ Community

Organization:

Program:

Identified Need, Problem, Situation	Service or Activity	Outcome	Indicator	Actual Results	Measurement Tool	Data Source	Frequency of Data Collection and Reporting
	Identify the # of clients to be served. Identify the time frame for the project. *May also include the # of units of service offered.*	General statement of results expected	Projected # of clients expected to achieve each outcome divided by the number served; the % expected to achieve	The Actual # of clients achieving the outcome, divided by the number served; the % of clients who achieved each outcome.		Include Collection Procedure, Personnel Responsible	
(1) Planning	(2) Intervention	(3) Benefit	(4) Performance	(5) Performance	(6) Accountability	(7) Accountability	(8) Accountability

Mission:

Proxy Outcome:

Participant Manual, "Introduction to ROMA" Version 5.0 © 2012 F. Richmond and B. Mooney, The Center for Applied Management Practices. Modified, from material © 1997- 2011, The Center for Applied Management Practices. Camp Hill, PA 717-730-3705, www.appliedmgt.com.

Logic Model Checklist

You can use this checklist to support evaluation of the logic model.

- ❑ Was the <u>mission</u> of the organization or program identified?

- ❑ Was a <u>Family, Agency, or Community</u> box checked?

- ❑ Is the <u>problem, need, or situation</u> statement clear? Column 1

- ❑ Does the <u>service or activity match the need</u>? Columns 1-2

- ❑ Was the <u>timeframe</u> realistic? Column 2

- ❑ Does the <u>outcome indicator match the outcome</u>? Columns 3-4

- ❑ Do the <u>outcomes and outcome indicators match the service or activity</u>? Columns 2,3,4

- ❑ Are the outcomes and outcome indicators <u>measurable</u>? Columns 3-4

- ❑ Are the outcomes and outcome indicators <u>realistic, clear, and attainable</u>? Columns 3-4

- ❑ Are the <u>target projections</u> for the outcome/indicators <u>realistic, clear, and attainable</u>? Column 4

- ❑ *(After the service has been completed)* Are the <u>*actual results consistent with the projected outcomes*</u>? *Column 5*

- ❑ Was a specific <u>measurement tool(s) identified</u>? Column 6

- ❑ Were all <u>sources of data identified</u>? Column 7

- ❑ Are the data <u>collection procedures and personnel specific</u>? Column 7

- ❑ Is the <u>frequency</u> of data collection sufficient to support weekly, monthly, or quarterly reporting? Column 8

- ❑ Is the logic model complete (Are columns 1-4 and 6-8 complete if you are in the planning mode? *If you have results, is Column 5 complete?*

- ❑ Is any additional information needed beyond what is in the logic model?

Participant Manual, "Introduction to ROMA" Version 5.0 © 2012 F. Richmond and B. Mooney, The Center for Applied Management Practices. Modified, from material © 1997- 2011, The Center for Applied Management Practices. Camp Hill, PA 717-730-3705, www.appliedmgt.com.

Using the Logic Model
To Assess Client Outcomes and Program Effectiveness

In the logic model on the next page, <u>Emergency Housing 1.0</u>, the agency's mission is: To ensure that all families have access to safe, clean shelter.

Column 1 documents a specific need: "Families are at risk of being evicted or are homeless."

Two services/interventions are provided: one month emergency rent payment and emergency shelter placement. <u>The assumptions behind the program are that issuance of a rent check or admittance to the shelter, automatically assures 30 days of safe shelter.</u>

The agency projected it would serve <u>200 families,</u> of which150 would receive emergency rent payment and 50 would receive emergency shelter placement. It projected that 100% of these families would achieve 30 days of stability.

An analysis of the outcome data (the results in Column 5) indicates that the <u>emergency shelter service is operating as it was expected to</u>.

o It was producing the outcome indicator that was projected.

However, the <u>emergency rent payment service was not as effective</u>.

o It produced a 92% outcome in the first 30 days. This is close to the projection at this point in time (30 days post service).

o <u>Follow-up data at 60 days reveals that not all of those who achieved 30 days stability were able to maintain it;</u> 85% remain in their homes after 60 days.

o At 90 days, families increasingly lose their housing; 58% remain in their homes after 90 days.

Participant Manual, "Introduction to ROMA" Version 5.0 © 2012 F. Richmond and B. Mooney, The Center for Applied Management Practices. Modified, from material © 1997- 2011, The Center for Applied Management Practices. Camp Hill, PA 717-730-3705, www.appliedmgt.com.

ROMA Logic Model 1.0 – Emergency Housing Example
National ROMA Peer-To-Peer Training Program

Organization: CAA **Program:** Emergency Housing ☑ Family ☐☐ Agency ☐☐ Community

Identified Problem, Need, Situation	Service or Activity — Identify the # of clients to be served. Identify the time frame for the project. *May also include the # of units of service offered.*	Outcome — General statement of results expected	Indicator — Projected # of clients expected to achieve each outcome divided by the number served; the % expected to achieve	Actual Results — The **Actual** # of clients achieving the outcome, divided by the number served; the % of clients who **achieved** each outcome.	Measurement Tool	Data Source — Include Collection Procedure, Personnel Responsible	Frequency of Data Collection and Reporting
(1) Planning	**(2) Intervention**	**(3) Benefit**	**(4) Performance**	**(5) Performance**	**(6) Accountability**	**(7) Accountability**	**(8) Accountability**
Families are at risk of being evicted.	200 families will receive housing assistance, during fiscal year July 1 to June 30			203 families actually received housing assistance, July 1, 2007 - June 30, 2008			
	One month emergency rent payment will be issued for 150 families.	Families remain in their own residence.	150 of 150, or 100%, of families remain in their own residence 30 days.	142 of 155, or 92%, of families remain in their own residence 30 days.	Housing application (for date of request).	Case record. Data entered into automated case record at time of encounter. Data entered by CAA case-manager.	Data collected at time of encounter. Summary report generated to supervisor daily. Weekly report generated to department head each Monday. Monthly report generated for executive director.
				132 of 155, or 85%, of families remain in their own residence 60 days.	Housing activity log showing payments.		
				90 of 155, or 58%, of families remain in their own residence 90 days	Record of paying rent Client report.		
Families are homeless.	Emergency shelter will be provided for 50 families.	Homeless families obtain emergency shelter.	50 of 50, or 100%, of homeless families obtain emergency shelter lasting no longer than 30 days.	48 of 48, or 100%, of homeless families obtain emergency shelter lasting no longer than 30 days.	Shelter log. Client report	Case Record. Data entered into case record at time of encounter. Data entered by shelter case-manager.	Data collected at time of encounter. Daily electronic report emailed to CAA at daily close of business.

Mission: To ensure that all families have access to safe, clean shelter. ▶ **Proxy Outcome:** None.

104

Participant Manual, "Introduction to ROMA" Version 5.0 © 2012 F. Richmond and B. Mooney, The Center for Applied Management Practices. Modified, from material © 1997- 2011, The Center for Applied Management Practices. Camp Hill, PA 717-730-3705, www.appliedmgt.com.

Program Evaluation and Program Improvement

This CAA used the logic model to <u>document</u> the emergency housing program results and to monitor performance. Collecting and analyzing follow-up outcome/performance data <u>revealed the limits</u> of the intervention and suggested that other factors may be adversely affecting families in the community.

The logic model, <u>Housing Assistance 2.0,</u> documents an <u>expanded need</u> <u>resulting from analysis of data in the 1.0 logic model</u>. Because of this analysis, the CAA <u>revised its mission,</u> <u>added interventions, and is now</u> <u>expecting additional outcomes</u>.

These outcomes are characterized with <u>the added dimension of time</u> represented by <u>short, intermediate, and long term</u>.

The agency identified additional funding to provide the newly added interventions to <u>50 of the clients from its total population of 200</u>. It felt that these clients would come from the emergency rent service. However, this is not identified on the logic model. The agency left this vague so that the additional services could also be available to the clients from emergency shelter, as it did not know who would be interested in the additional services.

Use of this logic model demonstrates a CAA's <u>responsiveness to data</u> <u>analysis</u> and its effectiveness in handling change and obtaining results.

This is "community action"!

Participant Manual, "Introduction to ROMA" Version 5.0 © 2012 F. Richmond and B. Mooney, The Center for Applied Management Practices. Modified, from material © 1997- 2011, The Center for Applied Management Practices. Camp Hill, PA 717-730-3705, www.appliedmgt.com.

ROMA Logic Model 2.0 – Housing Assistance Example
National ROMA Peer-To-Peer Training Program

Organization: CAA **Program: Housing Assistance** ☑ Family ☐☐ Agency ☐ Community

Identified Problem, Need, Situation	Service or Activity — Identify the # of clients to be served. Identify the time frame for the project. *May also include the # of units of service offered.*	Outcome — General statement of results expected	Indicator — Projected # of clients expected to achieve each outcome divided by the number served; the % expected to achieve	Actual Results — The Actual # of clients achieving the outcome, divided by the number served; the % of clients who achieved each outcome.	Measurement Tool	Data Source — Include Collection Procedure, Personnel Responsible	Frequency of Data Collection and Reporting
(1) Planning	**(2) Intervention**	**(3) Benefit**	**(4) Performance**	**(5) Performance**	**(6) Accountability**	**(7) Accountability**	**(8) Accountability**
	200 families will receive housing assistance, during fiscal year July 1 - June 30			203 families actually received housing assistance. 7/11/07-6/30/08			
Families are at risk of being evicted.	One month emergency rent payment will be issued for 150 families.	**Short Term** Families remain in their own residence.	**Short Term** 150 of 150, or 100%, of families remain in their own residence 30 days.	**Short Term** 142 of 155, or 92%, of families remained in their own residence 30 days. 132 of 155, or 85%, of families remained in their own residence 60 days. 90 of 155, or 58%, of families remained in their own residence 90 days	Housing application (for date of request). Housing activity log showing payments. Record of paying rent Client report.	Case record. Data entered into automated case record at time of encounter. Data entered by CAA case-manager.	Data collected at time of encounter. Summary report generated to supervisor daily. Weekly report generated to department head each Monday. Monthly report generated for executive director.
Families are homeless.	Emergency shelter will be provided for 50 families.	**Short Term** Homeless families obtain emergency shelter.	50 of 50, or 100%, of homeless families obtain emergency shelter lasting no longer than 30 days.	48 of 48, or 100%, of homeless families obtained emergency shelter lasting no longer than 30 days.	Shelter log. Client report	Case Record. Data entered into case record at time of encountered by shelter case mgr.	Data collected at time of encounter. Daily report emailed to CAA at daily.
Families need additional services to maintain housing. *(After 90 days,* *42% of the families lose their residence.)*	Additional intermediate and long term services provided to 50 Families (30 to 270 days): Transitional housing will be provided to 30 families.	**Intermediate** Families secure temporary subsidized housing.	**Intermediate Term** 30 of 50, or 60% of families obtain and remain in transitional housing	**Intermediate Term** 32 of 65, or 49%, of families obtain and remained in transitional housing.	Approved Housing Application for Transitional Housing. Housing records Client report.	Case record. Data entered into automated case record at time of encounter, by CAA case-manager.	Weekly report to department head each Monday. Monthly report for executive director.
	Housing Assistance (30 to 360 days) Arrangements made for public housing for 15 families and for unsubsidized rental housing for 4 families. Pre-purchase counseling for 1 family	**Long Term** Families obtain permanent housing.	**Long Term** 15 of 50 or 30%, of families secure public housing; 4 of 50, or 7%, obtain unsubsidized rental housing, 1 of 50, or 2%, purchased a home.	**Long Term** 12 of 65 or 18%, of families secured public housing; 15 of 65, or 23%, obtained unsubsidized rental housing, 0 of 65 purchased a home.	Lease Payment of rent Client report. Mortgage. or other closing documents.	City public housing records or private **landlord** reported to CAA case-manager.	Reported to CAA case-manager supervisor monthly, quarterly reports to executive director.

Mission: To ensure that all families have access to safe, clean shelter and to help families obtain safe, affordable permanent housing

Proxy Outcome: None.

Participant Manual, "Introduction to ROMA" Version 5.0 © 2012 F. Richmond and B. Mooney, The Center for Applied Management Practices. Modified, from material © 1997- 2011, The Center for Applied Management Practices. Camp Hill, PA 717-730-3705, www.appliedmgt.com.

ROMA Logic Model – S, I, L dimensions
National ROMA Peer-To-Peer Training Program

☐ Family ☐ Agency ☐ Community

Organization:

Program:

Identified Problem, Need, Situation	Service or Activity Identify the # of clients to be served. Identify the time frame for the project. *May also include the # of units of service offered.*	Outcome General statement of results expected	Indicator Projected # of clients expected to achieve each outcome divided by the number served; the % expected to achieve	Actual Results The <u>Actual</u> # of clients achieving the outcome, divided by the number served; the % of clients who <u>achieved</u> each <u>outcome.</u>	Measurement Tool	Data Source Include Collection Procedure, Personnel Responsible	Frequency of Data Collection and Reporting
(1) Planning	(2) Intervention	(3) Benefit	(4) Performance	(5) Performance	(6) Accountability	(7) Accountability	(8) Accountability
		Short Term	Short Term	Short Term			
		Intermediate Term	Intermediate Term	Intermediate Term			
		Long Term	Long Term	Long Term			

Mission:

Proxy Outcome: None.

Participant Manual, "Introduction to ROMA" Version 5.0 © 2012 F. Richmond and B. Mooney, The Center for Applied Management Practices. Modified, from material © 1997- 2011, The Center for Applied Management Practices. Camp Hill, PA 717-730-3705, www.appliedmgt.com.

Other Applications of the Logic Model

Activity – Create a housing outcome scale using the "Housing Assistance Logic Model" from previous pages.

Instructions: Review Column 1, the Need Statement and Columns 3 and 4 of the Logic Model 2.0, which were just presented. There are seven possible housing conditions that can be placed in the benchmarks. You should find conditions for all five benchmarks to create your Scale.

Outcome Level:　　　　☑ **Family** ☐ **Agency** ☐ **Community**

Benchmarks	Housing Scale Outcomes
Thriving Independent	
Safe Independent	
Stable Independent	
	Prevention Line
Vulnerable Dependent	
In-Crisis Dependent	

Hint: It is often helpful to view the top end of the scale as the "best" case scenario, and the lowest end of the scale as the "worst" case scenario.

Participant Manual, "Introduction to ROMA" Version 5.0 © 2012 F. Richmond and B. Mooney, The Center for Applied Management Practices. Modified, from material © 1997- 2011, The Center for Applied Management Practices. Camp Hill, PA 717-730-3705, www.appliedmgt.com.

Setting Targets

We have discussed the need for creating projections (targets) and reviewed established and recognized performance standards for baseball and selected industries.

The logic model can be a useful tool in the process of establishing realistic performance targets for our programs and services.

The logic model of an Adult Basic Education program on the next page identifies the activities and outcomes along with a numerical count that documents the steps in the program from screening and placement to achieving competency in basic math, reading and writing skills as measured by a TABE or receipt of a GED.

The following is the program service and outcome data for analysis:

- 100 persons – Recruited
- 95 persons – Screened, placed/enrolled. Five (5) dropped out during the screening/enrolling process
- 80 persons – Attended classes within guidelines. Fifteen (15) persons dropped out after screening/placement/enrollment and did not attend classes.
- 60 persons – Completed A.B.E. classes within 1½ years of enrollment. Twenty (20) persons did not attend classes within absenteeism guidelines and either dropped out or were dismissed.
- 35 persons – Achieved competency by TABE or GED Test, passed test and receive certification/diploma. Twenty-five (25) persons who completed all classes did not pass their tests.

Documentation of the program indicates a 35% success rate (35/100). Of all persons recruited into the program, 35% successfully achieve the outcome, passing the test <u>and</u> receiving certification/diploma. All the other program statistics were activity, not outcomes. If this program consistently produced the same results <u>and</u> the agency tracked both the activities and the outcomes, <u>a performance standard of 35% could be established for this program.</u> This performance standard would be a realistic measure of excellence such as demonstrated in baseball.

Participant Manual, "Introduction to ROMA" Version 5.0 © 2012 F. Richmond and B. Mooney, The Center for Applied Management Practices. Modified, from material © 1997- 2011, The Center for Applied Management Practices. Camp Hill, PA 717-730-3705, www.appliedmgt.com.

ROMA Logic Model 3.0 – A.B.E. Example for Setting Targets

Program: Adult Basic Education

☑ Family ☐ Agency ☐ Community

Identified Problem, Need, Situation	Service or Activity Identify the # of clients to be served (or the # of units of service offered). Identify the time frame for the project.	Outcome General statement of results expected	Indicator Projected # and % of clients to achieve each outcome	Measurement Tool	Data Source and Collection Procedures	Frequency of Data Collection and Reporting
(1) Planning	(2) Intervention	(3) Benefit	(4) Performance	(6) Accountability	(7) Accountability	(8) Accountability
Customer does not have basic math, reading, and writing skills.	**Short Term Outputs** 100 customers are recruited for placement into A.B.E. (Adult Basic Education) classes within first month of program year. 95 of 100 are screened and placed in A.B.E. classes within 30 days of intake and assessment. 80 of 100 attend A.B.E. classes within absenteeism guidelines for 90 consecutive days.		Performance	Accountability Agency Case Record contains screening results. Attendance log	Accountability Agency Community College	Accountability Reports within 30 days of intake and assessment. Quarterly
	Intermediate Term Output Completes attendance requirements for A.B.E. classes during 9-month program year.	**Intermediate Term Outcome** Achieves increased skills in identified academic area.	60 of 100, or 60% of customers, complete A.B.E. classes within 1½ years of enrollment and demonstrate an increase in academic skills.	Agency Case Record Teacher-made or textbook exams	Agency Community College	Quarterly
		Long Term Outcome Demonstrates competency in basic math, reading, and/or writing skills. Receives certificate, high school diploma, or other certification.	35 of 100, or 35% of customers, demonstrate ability to use increased skills/competence (by passing test or achieving certification) within 1½ years of enrollment.	TABE or GED Test Other Certification or Certificate	Community College Agency	Quarterly

Mission: To provide skill development and classes in basic math, reading, and writing to help customers become academically functional.
*****Please Note: Column 5, Actual Results, is missing from this logic model. This is the "planning" version, which is projecting the plan for your agency.

Participant Manual, "Introduction to ROMA" Version 5.0 © 2012 F. Richmond and B. Mooney, The Center for Applied Management Practices. Modified, from material © 1997- 2011, The Center for Applied Management Practices. Camp Hill, PA 717-730-3705, www.appliedmgt.com.

Introduction to the eLogic Model®

While the traditional logic model advances and clarifies thinking about Needs, Interventions, and Outcomes, as a "paper" tool it is difficult to aggregate information across multiple logic models.

It does not have the power of an electronic database.

If the logic units are <u>predefined</u> in a database, they become more useful to the agency's management. There are many possible ways to use software to assist in making the agency data more accessible for analysis.

One example:

The e-Logic Model® is an "electronic," or software driven, adaptation of the logic model and <u>supports a database of information gathering about agency performance</u>.

This electronic version of the logic model links "logic units" in program operations, (mission, need, intervention, projected results, actual results), and "logic units" in program accountability (measurement tool, data source, and frequency of data collection and reporting, including personnel assigned to function).

The "logic units" are assembled in a multi-column table, like the ones you have just worked with.

The eLogic Model® was developed by The Center for Applied Management Practices, Inc.

Participant Manual, "Introduction to ROMA" Version 5.0 © 2012 F. Richmond and B. Mooney, The Center for Applied Management Practices. Modified, from material © 1997- 2011, The Center for Applied Management Practices. Camp Hill, PA 717-730-3705, www.appliedmgt.com.

Introduction to the eLogic Model® - continued

The eLogic Model® includes a **"Knowledge Base"** organized into various "Domains." Within each domain, there are the appropriate **Needs, Services, and Outcomes.**

The domains correspond to the service categories in the CSBG language.

By "pre-loading" the Knowledge Base with content for Needs, Services, and Outcomes, the program manager has access to a <u>uniform database</u> from which to create a custom logic model.

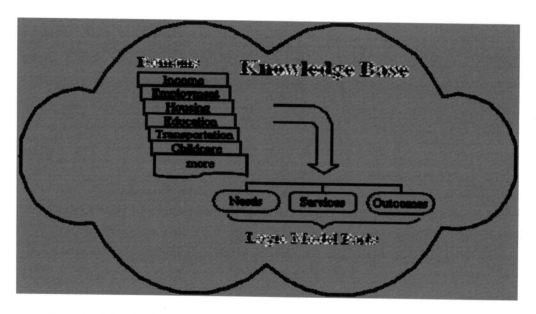

The sample eLogic Model® on the following page presents the same Housing Program depicted previously, but has check boxes where those items that pertain to a specific program or service can produce a specific logic model for the agency use.

The eLogic Model® uses either check boxes or dropdown combo boxes to custom select items from a program logic model that pertain to a particular program or service.

The sample is from the eLogic Model® currently used by the U.S. Department of Housing and Urban Development (HUD).

Participant Manual, "Introduction to ROMA" Version 5.0 © 2012 F. Richmond and B. Mooney, The Center for Applied Management Practices. Modified, from material © 1997- 2011, The Center for Applied Management Practices. Camp Hill, PA 717-730-3705, www.appliedmgt.com.

Sample eLogic Model® for Housing – Family

Identified Problem, Need or Situation	Service/Activity/Output Projected	Results	Outcome/Indicator Projected	Results
1	2	3	4	5
Planning	**Intervention**		**Impact**	
☐ **Individual or family is homeless** ☐ **Individual or family is at risk of losing their housing** ☐ **Individual or family lives in unsafe or unaffordable housing.**	Individuals or families receive housing services: ☐ Emergency shelter ☐ Hotel ☐ Temporary housing ☐ Transitional housing ☐ Domestic shelter ☐ Subsidized housing ☐ Public housing ☐ Section 8 housing ☐ Non-subsidized housing ☐ Mobile home ☐ House Individuals and families receive supportive services: ☐ Emergency rent payments ☐ Emergency mortgage payments ☐ Emergency vendor payments ☐ Utility or fuel Assistance ☐ LIHEAP ☐ Budget classes ☐ Housing counseling ☐ Case management ☐ Referrals to CCCS		Individuals or families are able to remain in their own homes or obtain more permanent housing: ☐ Prevent homelessness ☐ Emergency shelter ☐ Hotel ☐ Temporary housing ☐ Transitional housing ☐ Domestic shelter ☐ Subsidized housing ☐ Public housing ☐ Section 8 housing ☐ Non-subsidized housing ☐ Mobile home ☐ House	

Mission Statement: To ensure that individuals and families do not become homeless and have access to safe, affordable permanent housing.

A more thorough description, as well as a "flash" or automated demonstration of the eLogic Model®, can be found by going to The Center for Applied Management Practices, Inc. web site at, www.appliedmgt.com or www.elogicmodel.com.

113

Participant Manual, "Introduction to ROMA" Version 5.0 © 2012 F. Richmond and B. Mooney, The Center for Applied Management Practices. Modified, from material © 1997- 2011, The Center for Applied Management Practices. Camp Hill, PA 717-730-3705, www.appliedmgt.com.

J10			fx

eLogic Model®

OMB Approval 2535-0114 exp. 08/31/2014

Applicant Legal Name	0	
CCR Doing Business As Name	0	
HUD Program	HCVFSS	
Program Component	0	
Project Name		

DUNS No. 0 - 0 0

	Reporting Period	Year 1
	Reporting Start Date	
	Reporting End Date	2012

HUD Goals	Policy Priority	Needs	Services/Activities		Measures			Outcomes		Measures			Evaluation Tools
		2	3		4			5		6			7
	Policy	Planning	Programming		Pre	Post	YTD	Impact		Pre	Post	YTD	Accountability
		There is a need to maintain on-going linkages to services and economic opportunities for existing FSS program participants in order to support their transition to employment and economic self-sufficiency.	Employment-Job retention activities |Persons		10	Persons		Employment-Employment obtained above minimum wage |Persons		4	#VALUE!		A. Tools for Measurement
						#VALUE!		Employment-Employment obtained part-time |Persons Employment-Full time equivalent (FTE) |FTE Employment-Job placement |Persons Employment-Maintain employment for six months--one ye Employment-Maintain employment for three--six months Employment-Maintain employment greater than one year Employment-Promotion resulting in increased hourly wage			#VALUE!		Database Intake log
						#VALUE!					#VALUE!		Outcome scale(s)
						#VALUE!					#VALUE!		
						#VALUE!					#VALUE!		B. Where Data Maintained
						#VALUE!					#VALUE!		

Instructions | Coversheet | Year1 | Year2 | Year3 | Total | Services | GoalsPriorities | Needs | Outcomes | Tools | Reporting

HUD eLogic Model® - Housing Choice Voucher Family Self-Sufficiency Program - 2012

Participant Manual, "Introduction to ROMA" Version 5.0 © 2012 F. Richmond and B. Mooney, The Center for Applied Management Practices. Modified, from material © 1997- 2011, The Center for Applied Management Practices. Camp Hill, PA
717-730-3705, www.appliedmgt.com.

What Services Produce Outcomes?

This is a question that is being asked of our network, and it is difficult for us to be able to respond. Part of the difficulty is that some outcomes are the result of multiple services and some services produce multiple outcomes.

What is the most effective combination of services that is needed for a customer to achieve the outcome "got a job?" or "maintained a job for 60 days?"

Consider this research-based conclusion (Jan. 2011, Center for Law and Social Policy)

"A key aspect of the Annie E. Casey Foundation Center for Working Families model is that programs bundle and sequence services rather than offering just one component, or offering multiple components but leaving it up to participants to discover and seek out additional services. The hope is that the services will have a more-than-additive effect in promoting economic security, enabling clients to resolve immediate crises, acquire skills and credentials, get better jobs, and build the savings needed to prevent the next crisis and build for the future. Early evidence indicates that clients who receive bundled services are three to four times more likely to achieve a major economic outcome (such as staying employed, earning a vocational certification or associate's degree or buying a car) than clients receiving only one type of service. Delivering integrated services requires well-planned program design, the hiring and training of staff with strong skills and backgrounds, and the thoughtful use of technology and data collection. "

This "bundling of services" is one of the key strengths provided to CAAs by the CSBG funding stream.

The CSBG network could use the eLogic Model®, or other similar database programs, to analyze our service and outcome patterns to determine if we can show the same results as the Center for Law and Social Policy report indicated.

Participant Manual, "Introduction to ROMA" Version 5.0 © 2012 F. Richmond and B. Mooney, The Center for Applied Management Practices. Modified, from material © 1997- 2011, The Center for Applied Management Practices. Camp Hill, PA 717-730-3705, www.appliedmgt.com.

Closing

Implementing the ROMA Cycle

Next Steps...

Reinventing Organizations

Ten Questions Revisited

Participant Evaluation

Learning Objectives

- Participants recognize that they need to devise a plan to help their agencies, state systems, and the CSBG network implement ROMA.
- The Ten Questions are an example of a pre-post measure of increased knowledge.

117

Participant Manual, "Introduction to ROMA" Version 5.0 © 2012 F. Richmond and B. Mooney, The Center for Applied Management Practices. Modified, from material © 1997- 2011, The Center for Applied Management Practices. Camp Hill, PA 717-730-3705, www.appliedmgt.com.

Implementing the ROMA Cycle

Some things to consider as you move to implement ROMA.

- Gain commitment of all stakeholders including the Board, Executive Director, management, and staff for the full implementation of ROMA.

- Recognize that agency strategies, services, and activities must be planned to achieve results which meet identified needs, considering available resources and designed to address the agency mission.

- Identify potential partnerships and collaborations with other community-based organizations and local government to support the work of Community Action. Where your CAA does not offer the service or have the resources, form a partnership or other collaborative effort in your community to ensure that your clients have access to needed services and resources.

- Work with other networks such as the United Way, faith-based groups, county-based human services, and community coalitions to share ROMA principles and practices.

- Develop outcomes for specific programs and services using the logic model. Use the logic models to develop a common management and reporting framework.

- Develop outcome scales and matrices for programs and services that support and assist the client through an incremental change process. Use scales for any self-sufficiency programs. Share the scales with other human service providers in your community.

- Develop an internal quality assurance process to support your agency's accountability.

- Work towards implementing a common client identifier and common client intake system.

- Identify the information that is needed to support on-going results oriented management and accountability. Develop your management information system (MIS) after you know what information you need.

- Integrate ROMA concepts and language into your agency's planning, evaluation, and reporting processes. Also integrate in human resource and fiscal policies and procedures.

Participant Manual, "Introduction to ROMA" Version 5.0 © 2012 F. Richmond and B. Mooney, The Center for Applied Management Practices. Modified, from material © 1997- 2011, The Center for Applied Management Practices. Camp Hill, PA 717-730-3705, www.appliedmgt.com.

Next Steps

CAAs and CSBG Eligible Entities Need to…

- recognize the nature of the ROMA process and how it affects all aspects of the management of your CAA, future funding and relationships to funders. Good managers, staff, board members, and funders want to know what outcomes are achieved and the return they are getting on their investment.

- recognize the focus is on outcomes and performance in addition to activities or outputs. The focus is on client outcomes and performance in addition to program outcomes. How did the client benefit as a result of our interventions and how does this compare to last year or another program?

- identify and collect appropriate and relevant needs assessment and outcome data. Baseline data are necessary to measure change. It is important to identify the agency's information needs in a ROMA environment. It is important to convey or market the outcomes or impact of the interventions outside the CAA.

- recognize the need to gather and report on different data sets for various funders. It is important for a CAA to develop common and acceptable outcome measures useful to all funders. This can be accomplished through additional collaborative and partnership arrangements.

- train staff and Board in ROMA practices. Staff need basic tools and technologies to successfully perform their job in this environment. Boards need to better understand how implementation of ROMA strengthens the quality of the management and accountability responsibilities of their CAA.

Participant Manual, "Introduction to ROMA" Version 5.0 © 2012 F. Richmond and B. Mooney, The Center for Applied Management Practices. Modified, from material © 1997- 2011, The Center for Applied Management Practices. Camp Hill, PA 717-730-3705, www.appliedmgt.com.

Reinventing Organizations*

1. What gets measured gets done.

2. If you do not measure results, you cannot tell success from failure.

3. If you cannot see success, you cannot reward it.

4. If you cannot reward success, you are probably rewarding failure.

5. If you cannot see success, you cannot learn from it.

6. If you cannot recognize failure, you cannot correct it.

7. If you can demonstrate results, you can win public support.

*Reinventing Government, David Osborne & Ted Gaebler, 1992. Addison-Wesley Publishing Company, Reading, MA 01867, (617) 944-3700 Ext. 2431.

Participant Manual, "Introduction to ROMA" Version 5.0 © 2012 F. Richmond and B. Mooney, The Center for Applied Management Practices. Modified, from material © 1997- 2011, The Center for Applied Management Practices. Camp Hill, PA 717-730-3705, www.appliedmgt.com.

The Ten Questions – Revisited

1. True or False: Community Action agencies (CAAs) most effectively evaluate their results by focusing on the activities supported exclusively by the Community Services Block Grant (CSBG).

2. True or False: CSBG funds are a dedicated funding stream to support the work of Community Action.

3. True or False: "ROMA" is the term for the required reporting of data to a state and the Federal government.

4. True or False: CAAs are expected to focus on moving individuals and families to self-sufficiency and on community transformation, in addition to providing services to low-income people.

5. True or False: CAA programs are designed so that clients who participate in their services achieve measurable results.

6. True or False: Analysis of the agency's results can be used to identify effectiveness and performance of an agency.

7. True or False: The use of "results" instead of "services" may reduce the agency's competitiveness and marketability because of low numbers of results reported.

8. True or False: Community Action Agencies select services to offer based on available funding, not necessarily on the identified community needs.

9. True or False: "Results Oriented Management and Accountability" (ROMA) is the CAA term for a range of agency operation and administrative activities in addition to reporting.

10. True or False: Implementing ROMA in your CAA will affect the planning and fiscal functions, but will not affect the way programs and services are delivered.

Answers:
1-False, 2-True, 3-False, 4-True, 5-True, 6-True, 7-False, 8-False, 9-True, 10-False.

Participant Manual, "Introduction to ROMA" Version 5.0 © 2012 F. Richmond and B. Mooney, The Center for Applied Management Practices. Modified, from material © 1997- 2011, The Center for Applied Management Practices. Camp Hill, PA 717-730-3705, www.appliedmgt.com.

Made in the USA
San Bernardino, CA
16 March 2019